D0821388

THE CROSS AND THE CRISIS

THE
CROSS
AND THE
CRISIS

FULTON JOHN SHEEN

Essay Index Reprint Series

BOOKS FOR LIBRARIES PRESS
FREEPORT, NEW YORK

BX
1753
S52

First Published 1938
Reprinted 1969

Nihil obstat: H. B. RIES, Censor librorum
Imprimatur: ✚ SAMUEL A. STRITCH, Archiepiscopus Milwaukiensis
December 6, 1937

STANDARD BOOK NUMBER:

8369-1379-5

LIBRARY OF CONGRESS CATALOG CARD NUMBER:

73-99725

PRINTED IN THE UNITED STATES OF AMERICA

(CHASBOT COLLEGE LIBRARY)

HAYWARD, CALIFORNIA

Dedicated
to
Mary Immaculate
Mother of Our Saviour
Comforter of Our Afflicted World
In Token
of
Filial Love and Gratitude

67071

PREFACE

THE crisis facing the world today is political, economic, and religious: it is political, in the sense that parliamentarianism is giving way to dictatorship; it is economic, in the sense that finance and industry are being harnessed for social ends; it is religious, in the sense that the spiritual nature of man is challenged and denied. The thesis of this book is that the crisis is not so much political and economic, as it is moral and religious. The crux of the crisis is the cross.

This assertion immediately creates the problem: But has not Christianity failed? The answer to that depends upon the meaning one attaches to Christianity. Christianity may mean *historical* Christianity or Catholicism, or it may mean ethical or humanistic Christianity in all its thousand and one forms dating from the first sect of four hundred years ago to the latest of four hours ago. It is rather self-evident that for the past four hundred years Catholicism has been exiled from Western Civilization, not in the sense that it played no role in literature, art, politics, or science, but in the sense that the *spirit* of the modern world was definitely opposed to it. Now that the world has reached another great turning point in history, with the evaporation of milk-and-water Christianity, the minds of the present day are face to face, on the one hand, with Catholicism as the sole representative of Christianity and on the other with a completely secularized civilization. The choice before our generation is between an organic spiritual unity and an organized technical unity, or between a philosophy of life which says that man is a potential child of God and a philosophy of life which says that there is no God but Caesar. As Christopher Dawson has expressed it: "The new secularized civilization is not content to dominate the outer world and to leave man's inner life to religion; it claims the whole man."

This problem of the salvation of civilization and culture is treated in this book by an analogical treatment of the Parable of the Prodigal Son. If at times there is a statement of the failure of humanistic Christianity, it is not because there is any rejoicing at its failure in the camp of historical Christianity. Rather the failure is something to be regretted. A day is fast coming when Christians will have to unite in real Christianity to preserve it against the anti-Christian forces which would destroy it. For that reason, the refrain of this work is *not* that the political, or economic and financial solutions are unimportant, but rather that they are of secondary importance. What is all-important is spiritual regeneration. Social justice cannot be legislated into hearts; it is something which comes out of hearts, as the overflow of virtue and a good conscience. In other words, our ills will be cured by forces not involved in the crisis itself; namely, by the Divine.

The author wishes to express thanks to all who aided him in this work, and in particular to Messrs. E. I. Watkin, Christopher Dawson, and Nicholas Berdyaev.

CONTENTS

✿✿

Chapter I

SPIRITUAL BANKRUPTCY

A CERTAIN man had two sons: and the younger of them said to his father: 'Father, give me the portion of substance that falleth to me,' and he divided unto them his substance. And not many days after, the younger son, gathering all together, went abroad into a far country: and there wasted his substance, living riotously."

Such is the beginning of our Blessed Lord's story of the Prodigal Son. On hearing it, one of the first questions the human mind asks is why the young son should have been discontented at home and so anxious to leave it behind. From what the Gospel tells us after his return, it was probably a model home and a happy one. But before the consciousness of that truth dawned upon him by sad experience, the younger son thought that there was too much discipline and authority, that the father was perhaps not sufficiently modern, and above all else, too old-fashioned in his government of his children.

The younger son had probably said many times

1

that one must "sow his wild oats," and that the only reason we are put into this world is to enjoy it, and delight occasionally in the experience of a moral holiday. In any case, whether it was just the discipline of the father, or the restlessness of the young son who chafed under authority, the fact is, he made up his mind to shake himself free, to throw off the yoke, and to live his own life. He therefore asks for a division of property which was once held in common, for he now believes he can be a fountain of blessedness to himself and that by laying out his own life, he can make a far better investment than his father could have made for him. The father does not refuse the request, for it would have profited him nothing to have retained him at home against his will which was already estranged. It was a human example of the Heavenly Father who has given us the gift of freedom, and having given it, refuses to take it away even when we misuse it. No free man can be made good against his will.

"And not many days after, the young son gathering all together," says the Gospel — a statement of the gradual apostasy of the heart. A man is still under his own control while he is fulfilling his own pleasures, but is not yet possessed by vices and sins. It takes some days to gather all these together, but once amassed, he sets out for a foreign country — and the only real foreign country is one in which God is not. At first, possessed of wealth, and enjoying the thrill of new-found freedom from a father's authority, the youth felt he had the key which opens the door of every pleasure.

The world is full of those who teach that it cannot be wrong to do what you like, provided you can pay for it. Vista after vista of bewitching loveliness opens itself before his eyes as a kind of fairyland, and the temptation to spring forward and plunge into still other fairylands becomes a part of him, and almost an irresistible part. With the lights blazing and the orchestra playing, the Bacchanalian dance of life goes on.

But these are the pleasures of a season, the passing madness of the Prodigal's delirious dream. Sin and its pleasures were given him only grudgingly, enough to tempt, enough to inflame and corrode for a whole life, but never enough to satisfy for a single day. The demand for pleasure was still there. The appetite grew by what it fed on, but the satisfaction with each pleasure diminished. It was like having an ever-increasing appetite and an ever-decreasing supply of food. Sin had promised rapture; it gave the only thing it had to give: its own disgusting presence.

Soon the Prodigal's youth is consumed, his strength sapped, his wealth devastated; satiety has seized him like a perpetual sickness; his sense of enjoyment is blunted, for disenchantment comes early, long before youth is over and the capacity for real joy is gone. The young man feels he has already killed every true pleasure within him. And so the day finally came when, in the language of the Gospel, he had "wasted his substance living riotously." What a story of a life, a plunge and a ruin, so completely told in a few words! The world had opened wide its arms, welcomed to its bosom this darling of fortune, and when it had wrung the last glittering coin from his hand, it dropped him like a stone in a pond, and forgot that he had ever existed.

The moral application of this parable is already implied in its telling, but there is a historical application which can be made, and one which reveals the spiritual experiences of the modern world. The younger son is Western Civilization.[1] In the sixteenth century, Western Civilization went to the Spiritual Father of Christendom, the Vicar of Christ, and asked for its share of the substance: precious capital[2] of wisdom and tradition garnered through sixteen centuries of trial, persecution, and prayer. For sixteen

---

[1] The term *Western Civilization* is used here to denote the spirit of a culture divorced from traditional Christianity, which is Catholicism. The Catholic Church still continued to live in Western Civilization but it was not permitted to be its inspiration.

[2] "Once Christian morals were a part of Western Civilization's spiritual wealth. Without them this civilization never would have been moved to play the role in cultural progress with which it is credited. In its social inheritance from both the Roman and Greek civilizations it was chiefly enriched by Christianity, because there came with the political power of Rome, the spiritual energy of Christianity, and there came with the spiritual power of Athens, the permanent association and domination of the masses by Christianity. Briefly, Christianity gave the European his 'soul.' " L. Freund, *The Threat to European Culture*, pp. 20, 52 (New York: Sheed and Ward).

centuries this Spiritual Father had been preserving the great capital bequeathed by Christ, enriched by the teachings of the Apostles, the tradition of the Fathers, and the synthesis of the Scholastics. This patrimony was not always easy to keep. At times it was necessary to bleed for it, and even to die for it. It was a very precious kind of capital, not the capital of gold and silver, but something infinitely more precious: the capital of Divine Truths, such as the inspiration of Sacred Scripture, the necessity of a sacramental communion with Christ, the necessity of an infallible authority, the Divinity of Christ, the existence of God, and the necessity of religion.

Western Civilization, like the younger son, being free because human, could leave the father's house if it chose; and that it actually chose to do. With the inheritance under its arm in the shape of these all-important truths of religion, it went off into a foreign country, where there was no Spiritual Father to order and to command, but only individual whims and fancies. In the first wild moments of its freedom, there was nothing but the talk of independence. Children of Western Civilization who had broken with their Spiritual Father, prided themselves on having thrown off the "chains of Rome" and the "slavery of dogmas."[3] Carried away by false freedom,

----

[3] "The very fine things: humanism, nature, personal rights, human sociability, freedom, and science — the things for which we strove for centuries — degenerated and wasted away once they had been alienated from the Faith." — Ross Hoffman, *Restoration*, p. 134 (New York: Sheed and Ward).

Western Civilization began to spend the capital which the Spiritual Father had divided unto it. The history of the past four centuries is very briefly the history of that wasted capital: the patrimony of Christ committed to His Church. It was not all spent at once, nor was it all spent in the same place, nor with the same friends. Century by century the substance became smaller and smaller, and now as we look back in history, we can tell when each part of the capital was spent. In the sixteenth century, Western Civilization spent its belief in the necessity of authority; in the seventeenth century, it spent its belief in the authenticity of Sacred Scripture as the Word of God; in the eighteenth century, it spent its belief in the Divinity of Christ, the necessity of grace and the whole supernatural structure; in the nineteenth century, it squandered its capital of the existence of God as the Lord and Master and the Supreme Judge of the living and the dead. In our own day, it has spent its last penny: the belief in the necessity of a religion and obligation to a personal God. Truly, indeed, it has wasted its spiritual capital living riotously.

Two very important facts testify to this spiritual decline in Western Civilization; namely, mass-defection from Christ and mass-defection from God.

Mass-defection from Christ: In the sixteenth century practically everyone who left the Father's house believed firmly both in the divinity of Christ and the inspiration of Sacred Scripture. Within a century, some among them, starting with a rationalist principle, held, antecedent to all serious investigation, that there could be no such thing as the supernatural order; that the divinity of Christ was an illusion; and that a distinction had to be made between the Jesus of history and the Christ of faith. Within another century, more of the spiritual capital was spent and our Blessed Lord was reduced to a mere man among men. His office as Redeemer was ignored and theologians began to characterize Him as a "moral reformer" like Buddha and Confucius, Plato and Mohammed. Divines then began to speak of "adapting" Christ's idea to the times, and of freeing them from the "limitations" of His country and His narrower aspirations. Others went further and insisted on "revamping" the moral law to suit complex economic conditions.

How many of those sects which left the Spiritual Father of Christendom four centuries ago, believe today in the divinity of Christ? How many believe that He died on the cross as Redeemer of the world? Pick up the Sunday newspapers, and in most instances the sermons described therein discuss some purely social or economic topic, or else in vague terms describe our Blessed Lord as a man who taught humanitarian ethics. How many today believe that everything related by the Gospel concerning our Blessed Lord is true? How many believe His miracles, His Resurrection? How many believe His statements

concerning hell? How many accept His condemnation
of divorce? How many preach His Gospel of mortifica-
tion and penance? And yet three centuries ago there
was hardly a single one of those who left the Spiritual
Father of Christendom, who did not still retain such
beliefs. This is what is meant by mass-defection from
Christ. Thus the strange fact emerges from history
that Catholics, who have remained attached to the
Spiritual Father of Christendom, who were supposed
to be the great enemies of the Bible, are the only ones
actually supporting its authenticity and upholding its
inspiration. Catholics, who were supposed to be
hiding Christ under dogma, are the only ones who in
creed universally profess the divinity of that same
Christ. There is no test like time to prove undying
loyalty and devotion.

There is also mass-defection from God. Three centuries ago everyone who left the Father's House believed in the existence of God and the necessity of
religion, but within a century they were spending
some of that very precious capital. In the eighteenth
century the Deists, puffed up with scientific progress,
taught that God made the world, sent it into space,
and that from that day on, the world has been taking
care of itself. Within a century, men denied there
ever was a Creator, that He made a world, or that
there is such a thing as a heaven. The only God there
is, is the universe with its vague cosmic urge to attain
ever greater heights; what men before called God,

they now, in their new vision, call Nature. In our own day men speak of God, but they mean a "name for the ideal tendency in things"; they speak of religion, but they mean by it "service to humanity." Like merchants who continue to use old trade names to win the good will of their customers, they speak of religion and of God, but how many take a definite cognizance of God? How many believe in the Providence of God who watches over us with greater attention than He watches over the flight of a sparrow or the growth of a lily? How many believe in the existence of a Perfect Being, whose Essence is Knowledge and Love? How many today believe even in the Deist position that there is a God in the heavens? And yet one hundred and fifty years ago most of those who left the Father's House believed these things. Examine the writings in some old American colleges, such as Harvard, William and Mary, and Yale, and you will find that even a hundred years ago most of their professors not only believed in a personal God, but had a genuine devotion and love of Him.[4] Of how many in these same institutions can the same be said today? How many even believe they have a soul to save? Thus again the startling fact emerges that Catholics who were supposed to be the great enemies of reason, who were supposed to be stifling it with authority, are today the only ones who,

---

[4] Cf. James J. Walsh, *Education of the Founding Fathers of the Republic;* cf. also Daniel Gilbert, *Crucifying Christ in Our Colleges.*

as a body, believe that reason, unaided by faith, can come to a knowledge of God, His Wisdom, and His Power. Once more, time is the great test of loyalty and devotion.

The story of the past four hundred years is the story of a spiritual decay and the squandering of the substance of Divine Truth. Christ, who is God, has been reduced to a mere man. Man, who is made to the image and likeness of God, has been reduced to a mere animal; and an animal has been reduced to a mere atom. This is called "Progress!" Is it any wonder that thoughtful men are beginning to write and speak of the Decline of the West? Spengler, Massis, and a host of others, are right in saying that our Western world is on the decline. Many of them are wrong only in their explanation.[5] It is not

---

[5] "To accept Spengler's fatalistic thesis that every culture after a certain period of time is doomed to expire is to paralyze our strength needed for the great tasks ahead. One of the strongest motives for human conduct and thought is *Hope*. Men seldom dare to view facts in the cold, clear light of day. . . . *Every* culture, however, is the work of man, and man is incapable of realizing his dream of a perfect society on earth. Whatever program is embarked on, whether socialist or capitalist, aristocratic or democratic, the decisive factor is the character and the ability of the men in power. But the men in power, under any system, are few; and their ability and character are not revealed to the masses until they have made good use of their power for good or for ill; and since we are all human, no political or economical world order can overcome the power of evil. Participators in an exhausted culture, above all, the distressed classes in a declining epoch, will always clutch at fresh hopes with all their remaining strength. If religion and the representation of the next life fail to satisfy their materialistic desires, they dream of a new culture, of the final victory of absolute justice and goodness in *this* world." —

machinery, nor finance, nor naval armaments, nor the amassing of gold, nor rigorous iron laws of determinism, which have effected this decline. The two decisive factors in the breakdown of Western Civilization have been the two causes just mentioned: mass-defection from Christ and mass-defection from God.

The story of the Prodigal Son now enters into its second scene. It is now the hour of disillusionment. While the lights were blazing, this world seemed to be the only world worth living in, and the only world of which he could be sure. But these were just enchanting dreams, and the characters of pleasure which had played their parts now passed across the stage never to be seen again. The curtain rang down. The good wine which the world offered him at first, it now offers him no longer. The world which once was at his feet now has changed its role, and evidently he is its slave. A hint is here of that awful mystery in the downward progress of souls by which he who begins using the world as a servant to minister unto his pleasures, must submit in the end to a reversion of the relations between them, so that now the world uses him as its servant, and sin as its slave. Some servants have to be kept in their place or they will

Ludwig Freund, *The Threat to European Culture*, pp. 122, 123 (New York: Sheed and Ward).

Nicholas Berdyaev, of the modern school of Russian thinkers, offers a profound analysis of the present-day social situation in his books, *Der Sinn der Geschichte, Christianity and Class War, The End of Our Time*, and *The Bourgeois Mind*.

control the master. The world is such a servant. Unless we are master of it, it will master us. The Prodigal now becomes cheap in the esteem of that world in whose service he has forfeited all. A terrible ennui palls his very soul. The bondage becomes greater and the power for throwing it off less. With desires always satisfied there is nothing left to be desired, until satiety becomes a persecutor. Like a sailor at sea made more thirsty by the salt water which he drinks, so the Prodigal was maddened by the very pleasures which he enjoyed. Sin was rich in its promises, but it gave the only thing it can give, and that is the death which dogs its footsteps. What a fall for the boy who had ridden forth in hope and beauty from the peaceful abundance of his father's house, "to enjoy life," "to be independent," and "to be free!"

And as our Lord tells the story, "there came a mighty famine in that country and he began to be in want!" There is always a famine in a far-off land which means away from the Father's House. Before the spirit is quite quenched and the soul wholly carnalized, there remains a craving for higher things, but when the spirit is quenched, there is a famine of even that false bread which is not bread, and a thirst for those stolen waters which only make the thirst more keen. The hunger is now of such a kind that it can no longer crave the food of virtue. It is that queer aftertaste of all the world's feasts: a distaste for what we have, and an abhorrence of that which we have not. At one stroke our Lord set it before us, compressing into a single sentence the history of all erring souls, the fate of all sinful nations and all sinful men — "And he went and cleaved to one of the citizens of that country. And he sent him into his farm to feed swine. And he would fain have filled his belly with the husks the swine did eat, and no man gave him to eat." "He would fain have filled his belly" — it is no longer a question of satisfying his appetite, but only of satisfying the lower part of himself. Only God can satisfy the real hunger, for no one can feed the heart but God. The poor Prodigal was, as it were, sitting down at the ashes of a palace which his own hands had burned. He was feeding on husks and he was still in want. It is a passage from ten thousand biographies, best expressed in the words Byron wrote at Missolonghi at the age of thirty-six, the year when a profligate existence brought his death.

> My days are in the yellow leaf;
> The flowers, the fruits of life are gone;
> The worm, the canker and the grief
> Are mine alone.
>
> The fire that on my bosom preys
> Is lone as some volcanic isle
> No torch is lighted at its blaze —
> A funeral pile!

Now to resume the interpretation of the Prodigal

Son in the light of spiritual experience in the modern world. Leaving the Father's House, Western Civilization gradually squandered its spiritual heritage, living well with the modern world, becoming popular with it by sacrificing its spiritual possessions for the sake of momentary applause.

Having wasted its substance riotously, a famine now arises in the land of Western Civilization, a famine not for bread of the body alone, but a famine for the bread of the spirit. There is a famine for certainty and guidance among those who spent the capital of their belief in Sacred Scripture; there is a famine for a helping hand more kindly than the human among those who spent belief in His divinity; there is a famine for Life and Truth and Love in those souls who spent belief in the Trinity. There is a famine for faith among those who doubt; a famine for love among those who war; and a famine for the supernatural among the humanists. This vast dissolution of the spiritual patrimony has left civilization with a feeling of emptiness like that which follows a fever or an unhappy love affair, in which trivial illusions are substituted for majestic faiths, and belief in progress for belief in God.

What happened to the religion of Western Civilization? The answer is to be found in the words: "and he went and cleaved to one of the citizens of that country." Like the Prodigal who, in the days of famine, cleaved to a citizen of the foreign country, so, too, does the religion of Western Civilization in the days of its spiritual famine attach itself to temporalities which are foreign to the service of God; it links itself up with things which are strange to religion, and to interests which are alien to the Kingdom of Heaven; it affiliates itself with worldly things which are alien to the things of Christ. Having wasted its capital and now being spiritually bankrupt, modern religion needs must live, and so it adheres to citizens of foreign countries.

Having lost Divinity, the religion of Western Civilization now ties itself up with a thousand worldly interests which are not of the essence of religion, such as politics, social reform, economics, drug control, and the liquor traffic. I am not saying that religion should not be interested in the things of Caesar, nor that it should be indifferent to politics, and social well-being, but I do say that these are not the primary concern of religion, nor that to which it owes first allegiance, any more than it can be said that the Prodigal owed greater allegiance to the citizen of a foreign country than to his own father. Religion is indeed in a foreign land when it is more interested in mental hygiene than in the forgiveness of sin; in politics rather than in prayer; in the theory of relativity rather than in the Absolute; in crime prevention rather than morals; and in sex rather than in God.

Fifty years ago the Church could depend upon the sects to help her defend some of the fundamental dogmas of Christianity, such as belief in God and the divinity of Christ; twenty-five years ago the Church could depend upon the sects to help her defend certain elementary moral truths such as the sanctity of the marriage tie and the commandments of God. Now the Church is fighting the battle practically alone. Having fallen away from dogmas the sects had only positive moral precepts left; these were abandoned for negative moral precepts. Today most sermons represent a general emotional appeal without any definite precepts or command which will make these emotions pass into Christian action during the week. Fifty years ago the Church was condemned as the enemy of reason; now she is condemned because she is the champion of reason, and insists that the existence of God is grounded not in a sentimental experience but in sound logic which reasons from the visible things of the world to the invisible God.

There is no reason for rejoicing in the decline of beliefs in those who left the Father's House. As a matter of fact, the world would be a thousand times better off today if they still held the beliefs they held when first they left the Church. Having surrendered the authority of the Church, they next gave up the authority of the Bible, and now if you ask a man outside the Church how he knows what is true, he will say: "I feel it in here." No longer are they frightened at their inexpertness in theology. Each one is his own court of appeal.

This spiritual bankruptcy of Western Civilization has created the much-discussed question: Has Christianity failed?[6] Why is it so many say: Christianity has

————

[6] "Against those today who claim that Christianity is a failure, both Christians and the history of the Church testify. The outward history of the Church can be seen by all, but her inward story of holiness cannot be so easily noted. As with individuals, so with society, men uncover the evil more readily than the good, for it is easier to learn the externals of our fellow men than to arrive at their inner selves. And so their spiritual struggles we ignore, and judge them by their outward actions, which often enough are spoiled by passion and sin. It is not fair to criticize Christianity for the sins of Christian men and women. Christianity has had a long struggle with the "old man" in overcoming heathenism, barbarity, the baser instincts, and in setting up the religion of love. Her work is not material, but spiritual, and naturally her tools and activities are spiritual. Her achievements we are able to see only with spiritual eyes not blinded by material dust.

"The Russian experiment is an attempt to do better than Christianity; and so far the results have been disappointing to themselves and the world at large. They have tried to get rid of evil and suffering and bring in justice. Their plan is breaking because it rests, not on human freedom, as they would like to think, but rather on the violation of it. Their compelling men to justice is the point of difference between Christianity and Communism. For the materialistic socialists there is no such thing as sin or the spiritual; their problem is the elimination of suffering and social injustice. They would force men to be good; but God does not compel men to be virtuous. He wants their freedom, and not just the outward victory of justice. In this sense God permits evil, and draws good from its workings."

As for the problem of suffering, "Christianity is the religion of the Cross, and it sees a meaning in suffering." To reach eternal happiness without suffering is an impossibility for the Christian. At bottom original sin and its effects for mankind must be understood, if we would know that the "so-called 'failure of Christianity' is a human failure and not a divine defeat." — Nicholas Berdyaev, *The Bourgeois Mind,* chapter on "The Worth of Christianity," *passim.*

On this topic see another work of his, *End of Our Time,* pp. 60 ff.; also Ross Hoffman, *Restoration,* pp. 124 ff., and 198, 199.

been tried and found wanting? Possibly the answer is, as Chesterton has suggested, that Christianity has been found hard, but never tried. The real answer, however, is to be found by divesting the term *Christianity* of its vague meaning. Christianity may mean either one of two things:

a) Christianity for some means a vague ethical brotherhood, a broad vacuous grouping of sects, teaching contrary and contradictory versions of Christ's teaching but generally limiting it to social service and general good fellowship. This type of Christianity only accepts as much of Christ's teaching as public opinion will approve, e.g., the law against murder, but rejects that part of the Master's teaching which public opinion will not approve, e.g., the law against divorce, or the eternal punishment for unrepented sin.

b) In contrast to this ethical Christianity or refined humanism there is *historical* Christianity or a social organism governed by one Head, professing the same Truths, vivified by the same Sacraments, and reaching back in unbroken continuity to Christ Himself. Historical Christianity is the Catholic Church, and from this point on, whenever the term *Church* is used, it means the Roman Catholic Church, which is the Mystical Body of Christ.

Now we are in a position to answer the question: Has Christianity failed? The answer is: If by the term *Christianity* is meant that vague ethical humanism which has repudiated practically all the divine elements in Christianity, then Christianity has failed.

The reasons why it has failed are many, but there are three generally given by non-Catholic leaders which are worthy of mention. The first is that the religion of Western Civilization, or Protestantism in all its forms, has identified itself with a social order which is definitely passing away. Any religion which "keeps up to the times" must be prepared to die with the times: the Modernism of 1938 is not the Modernism of 1939. In the words of H. Richard Niebuhr, Professor of Ethics at Yale University, "the church has adjusted itself too much rather than too little to the world in which it lives. It has identified itself too intimately with capitalism, with the philosophy of individualism, and with the imperialism of the West. . . . The captive church is the church which has become entangled with these systems of worldliness. It is a church which seeks to prove its usefulness to civilization, in terms of civilization's own demands."[7]

A second reason for the liquidation of non-Catholic Christianity is one closely allied to the foregoing; namely, the passing of individualism. This point will be stressed in a subsequent chapter. Suffice it to note presently, that the world has recently shifted its emphasis from the individual to the collective, and since the religion of Western Civilization was definitely individualistic in temper, it follows that it has

---

[7] *The Church Against the World*, pp. 3, 138 (Chicago: Willett, Cark and Co.).

lost the environment necessary for its growth. To quote Dr. Niebuhr again: "The question which we raise in this situation may be best stated in the gospel phrase: 'What must we do to be saved?' The 'we' in this question does not refer to our individual selves, as though we were isolated persons who could have a life apart from the church or apart from the nation and the race. It denotes rather the collective self, the Christian community. In an earlier, individualistic time evangelical Christians raised the question of their salvation one by one, and we cannot quarrel with them. Today, however, we are more aware of the threat against our collective selves than of that against our separate souls."[8]

Thirdly, the religion of Western Civilization or non-Catholic Christianity has gradually surrendered one Divine Truth after another, in an effort to effect a compromise with the world, with the result that it suits national cultures but not the cross of Christ. Francis P. Miller, chairman of the World Student Christian Federation and Professor of Church History in the University of Chicago, writes: "The precariousness of the position of Protestant churches consists in the fact that the nature of nationalism is such that it can isolate sections of the Protestant community and destroy these sections in detail." The Protestantism of Germany, he goes on in substance to state, suits the national culture of Germany, but not the national

---

[8] *Ibid.*, p. 2.

culture of France; the Protestantism of America suits the national culture of America, but not the national culture of England; and so on for the rest of the world. But this is not as it should be: "The Christian cross is not an American cross or a British cross or an Italian cross. It is the possession of any man of any race who understands its message and lives by faith in its transforming power. The reality which that cross reveals is not the by-product of a particular national culture or of a particular racial experience. On the contrary, that reality is utterly independent of the evolution or destiny of particular nations or races. These human collectives cannot by any virtue or wisdom of their own add one iota to the validity of its truth or subtract one iota from its validity. All a nation or a race can do is to live by that truth or reject it, and in either case the consequences of the choice must be borne.

"If the Bible and Western European culture were the most important sources of such universality as Protestantism possessed, it is obvious that the time has long since passed when either of these sources could be relied upon to continue to supply Protestants with a universal frame of reference. This fact consti-tutes the supreme crisis upon which the Protestant movement is now entering. The Protestant churches no longer have a common ground of unity, they do not teach truths which are equally valid for men everywhere, and as long as they do not teach such truths they cannot be regarded as reliable witnesses to the Christian faith."[9]

In answer, then, to the question: Has Christianity failed? the answer is in the affirmative, if by Christianity we mean the religion which has identified itself with the passing spirit of Western Civilization, and has gradually surrendered the divinity of Christ on His cross for the sake of being modern.

But if by Christianity, one means that historical organic Body of Life and Truth which has been the leaven in the world for 1900 years, or the Catholic Church, then Christianity has not failed. The Church, and by this we mean always the Catholic Church, has not been tried for 400 years; it has not even been considered. It has been *ignored*. The modern world knows less about it than the man in the moon, and it dispenses itself from a study of its claims for the same reason as the first hearers of Christ's message dispensed themselves from hearing His message: "Can anything good come out of Nazareth?" Ignorance can be accumulated just as well as wisdom, and during the past 300 years the world has accumulated a tremendous amount of ignorance concerning her. Through long centuries she has been outlawed and ignored, but she has never failed any more than Christ failed when His fellow citizens cast Him out of His home town of Nazareth. Her days of being ignored are over. She is now returning from exile.

---

[9] *Ibid.*, p. 73; cf. pp. 76, 89.

As Ross Hoffman has put it: "Ever since the exile of
the Church from the lives of many peoples at the time
of the Protestant Revolution, her activities were
narrowed more and more. Philosophy, economics,
science and ethics slipped from her influence. Even
where she remained established, her movements were
hampered by the State, as we can observe in the Catholic countries of Italy, Spain, and France, during the
eighteenth and nineteenth centuries when their
peoples were doubting the Church's adaptability to
Western Civilization. . . . Social and economic chaos,
broken morality, pessimism and starved souls are the
evils of the day that come in the wake of the Church's
banishment. Modern Civilization stands indicted, and
the Church cannot be implicated because she had
been sent into exile. Only when the Western mind
began to doubt its own insufficiency did the Faith
start to return from exile. And now thoughtful men
are beginning to realize that Catholicism has the
life food for our starving age."[10] The day is coming
when the world will once more begin to make distinctions, and instead of speaking of Christianity as a
vague term like religion, men will begin to use it
in the historical sense. They did not really hate the
Church, but only what they mistakenly believed to
be the Church. The vision of the Church then will
come to them as to one awakened in the watches of

_____

[10] R. J. S. Hoffman, *Restoration*, pp. 129–133; also p. 198 ff. (New York:
Sheed and Ward).

the night; they will see the dead walking and the blaze of that living spectacle will make them forget everything else but the glory of the Risen Christ.

The future will see no other religion than the divine historical religion of Christ and His Church. No potpourri of Eastern and Western religion will arise to satisfy the cry of the world. The human heart that has had one great love can never really have another. We have but one heart, and if we give it away we give away our deepest capacity for love. What is true of the individual is true of society. Society has used up a life's capacity for love in the great adventure of Christianity. Its bones are not too old to accustom themselves to new postures of worship. We have given our heart away once to the divinity of the Church; and we cannot give it away again. Hence the difference between the future and the present will not be a difference of religion, but a difference of attitude. People will no longer be ignorant of the Church; they will no longer be indifferent to it. They will see only two things: the living vine and the withered branches; the Father's House and the Prodigal's; they either will gather or they will scatter; they either will love or they will hate. That is why the world will end as Christianity began, namely, with a great and mighty battle between the world and the Church, between Baal and Christ, between the forces who crucify and the Power which is crucified.

This sad and tragic dissipation of spiritual capital

by the Western World does not necessarily mean the "Decline of the West." There is still a possibility of recovery, as there was for the Prodigal. The Prodigal never became a citizen of the foreign country. He was always a stranger there. There would have been no hope for him, however, if he had not felt himself an alien, or if he had made himself a citizen in that land of husks. And so, too, with Western Civilization. Were it untroubled by heavenly homesickness, were there no divine nostalgia, no remembrance of a Father's house, there would be no hope. But such is not the case. There is a feeling of being strangers in this land of religion which has forgotten the Divine; a feeling of uneasiness, a discontent with the husks they are given, and a hankering after a food that is more spiritual.

Western Civilization has cleaved to the things that are foreign, but has never become a citizen in that foreign land. There is no greater proof of this than the general attitude toward world conditions now as contrasted with the attitude of fifty or a hundred years ago. Up until the World War one could not pick up a book, or a magazine, or listen to a speech without hearing something about "Progress." Man was presumed to have been liberated from religious authority; democracy was presumed to have given him political liberty; evolution made his progress not only possible but certain; machinery eventually would relieve the world of poverty and disease;

67071

mutual trade relations would eliminate the causes of war; religion without dogmas would remove the intolerance of sects and dissolve all of them into a vague fellowship of good feeling. Everywhere there was Hope, Prosperity, a certain onward, upward march to the tune of evolution, to the Golden Age of material well-being and earthly happiness.

Then came the World War which turned the world into a slaughterhouse. The so-called civilized man who was supposed to be a descendant of the ape, now descended even below that level. The great Babels of earthly happiness built without the great Cornerstone came tumbling down on our heads. Visions of grandeur began to fade. A few years of prosperity gave a false hope for the success of the biological man as against the man called to supernatural destiny with God. And then came the Depression. The machine which was to make us all rich and happy made many poor and miserable. It produced more than the men which it displaced could buy. They were told to produce more, and then dismissed because they produced too much. Distribution broke down. The world had hoped for peace and it got wars and rumors of wars; it had promised prosperity, and got starvation in the midst of plenty; it had hoped to make the world safe for democracy, and got a democracy which was hardly safe for the world; it had promised a world free from authority, and got more authority than it ever had before. The result is that today

instead of progress, evolution, prosperity, and world
peace, we have decay, unrest, uncertainty, doubt, and
above all else a feeling of not knowing where we are
going. We were great believers in progress even
though we did not know where we were progressing.
The machine is blamed; progress is cursed and evolution is suspected. Man now crouches in fear from the
very terrors he himself has created.[11] He has set fire
to his own house, and now it tumbles involving him
in its ruins. And that whole school of false prophets
such as Wells, Shaw, and the like, are now resigned
to a philosophy which is hardly distinguishable from
despair. The map was thrown aside and the world
has lost its way.

But there is no reason for despair. However much
Western Civilization has been disillusioned, it still
feels itself in a foreign land. There is still some
remembrance of the Father's house. The world is
becoming logical; it is seeking a complete philosophy
of life and there are only two, both of which we shall
speak of in the next chapter. Suffice it to say here that
some are coming back again to God, not through the
preservation of their baptismal grace, but by a trial
of the world. They are dissatisfied in this foreign land
of husks. They have leaned on the staff of the economic and found it pierced their hands; they have
walked with the staff of science alone, and found it
a broken reed. Thus it is that they, like the Prodigal,

----

[11] Dawson, *Religion and the Modern State,* p. 116.

are witnessing against the world even though they are children of it. It is the blessed lot of those whose wanderings are thus overruled, to yearn for the banquets of the Father's house. It is a great gift that those having lost the free gift of God, regain it by His compulsory remedies, and who after having heard all the ramblings of skeptics and tasted the fleeting pleasures of an hour, now are made to cry out with Peter at Capharnaum, "Lord, to whom shall we go?"

It may take a long time for Western Civilization to realize that the good it is seeking, is the good that it left. Many heartaches and long, sad experiences were necessary before the Prodigal realized that the Father's House which he left was the only place where he could find peace and contentment. It took many a heartache to convince the Prodigal that the authority of the Father's house which he rejected was the only authority which could make him free. In like manner the world will not quickly realize that the Church, which it believed was so restraining to liberty, is really the only one that makes us free, and that which was thought so much behind the times, is the only institution which has survived the times.

However long the time it takes to learn this lesson, there is always present the consoling picture of the Father of the Prodigal. Daily that Father would go to a hill and look down all the roads to the foreign lands hoping almost against hope that he would catch a glimpse of his son. So, too, with the Spiritual Father of all Christendom; daily his eyes search the horizons of the foreign lands for Western Civilization which is already dying of famine for the things of the Spirit of God.

His Holiness, Pius XI, in most tender words of fatherly solicitude gives the modern Prodigal the invitation to return. Here we quote from the *Quadragesimo Anno:* "But We are far, indeed, from being exasperated by these injustices or dejected by Our pastoral sorrow. We have no wish to drive away or repel Our children who have been so unhappily deceived, and who are wandering so far from the paths of truth and salvation. On the contrary, We invite them with all possible solicitude to return to the maternal bosom of the Church. God grant that they listen to Our voice. God grant that whence they set out, thither they may return to their Father's House; that where their true place is, there they may return." But what if the Prodigal does not come back? What if he stay in that foreign land? What other things can he choose if he choose not to return to the Father's House? That question will be answered in the next chapter.

Chapter II

THE LAST BATTLE

AFTER the Prodigal had wasted his substance living riotously he "began to be in want." A famine was abroad in the land: a famine for spiritual truth and strength which once was his. He could find no other work save that of feeding the swine, and in the language of the parable, "he would fain have filled his belly with the husks the swine did eat; and no man gave him to eat."

In like manner, Western Civilization having squandered the great spiritual capital bequeathed to it by the Father of Christendom began to cleave to things which were foreign to the very nature of man and finally reached a point where it was concerned almost exclusively with the material and the economic. In other words, it filled its belly, not its soul, for it had almost forgotten there is a soul; not its mind, for it believed in Pragmatism and the relativity of truth; not its heart, for that had become hardened by the mad pursuit of wealth.

This represents a new stage in the decline. It is

one thing to squander; it is quite another thing to think only of satisfying the lower part of one's nature, and not that higher realm where the Spirit of God dwells. Western Civilization has squandered its capital; it has surrendered its belief in the supernatural and even the natural end of man; it is no longer witnessing a civil war between Christian sects, for the days of heresy are over. Minds are no longer isolating a truth from its organic whole, as one might tear an arm from a body, and making a religion out of it. Even the Church herself feels heresy is liquidating, for perhaps never before in her history was she so impoverished for want of good, sound, strong intellectual opposition, as she is at the present time. There are no foemen worthy of her steel. No longer is she called upon to discuss the problem of the alleged conflict of science and religion. The opposition has shifted from a world in which she had to uphold her divinity against sects which asserted they were divine, to a position where she has to uphold her divine character against those who deny Divinity.

A fragment, of course, of that spiritual capital is still floating about the world, for, to change the figure, our age is living in what might be called the penumbra of Christianity — that line where light fades out and shadows begin. All that is still sublime in philanthropy, is but a splinter of the cross of Calvary which the Church holds erect above the world; all that is noble and happy in marriage is a reflection from the

Church's teaching of the sanctity of two hearts and the honesty of a vow; all that is best in the justice and equity of governments, is a reflection of the Church's spiritual principle that we must render unto Caesar the things that are Caesar's, and unto God the things that are God's; and all that is satisfying in democracy is the principle that all are equal because redeemed by the precious Blood of our Saviour, Jesus Christ.

But apart from this reflection of Christian truth which is still dimly visible in the world, the great spiritual patrimony of the ages is gone. The Church with her finger on the pulse of contemporary civilization realizes it more than that moribund civilization itself realizes it. Ethical Christianity has failed. Western Civilization is not just suffering from a famine of spiritual values; it is not even caring about them. It is now seeking to stuff itself with the husks of the secular, the economic, the political, the worldly. This new thing which no longer is concerned with the soul, but with the belly, is *a philosophy of life which mobilizes souls for economic and secular ends,* a Caesarism or adoration of the State, a glorification of the human collective through the depersonalization of man, and a suffocation of human personality and its subsequent absorption into the mass. Sometimes it takes only the form of a race-worship such as Nazism and at other times the form of economic worship such as Communism. Inasmuch as the latter is endowed with a missionary activity and is bent on world revolution, we shall be concerned principally with it.

Communism is not a party, but a philosophy of life. A party is formed by the free adherence of members; a philosophy of life, on the contrary, imposes itself on the members; a party grows from the outside inward, like a crystal; a philosophy of life grows from the inside out, like a cell. A party keeps its finger on the pulse of suffrage to give what it wants: if the public wants ghosts, the party gives it ghosts. A philosophy of life is not guided by what the public wants, but by the principles of its philosophy. Christianity is a philosophy of life, because it lays claim to the whole man, offering him guiding principles not only for his body but for his soul. Communism, too, is a philosophy of life, in the sense that it, too, lays claim to the whole man, but man according to its principles is only a creature of the earth, and not also a potential member of the Kingdom of God in the world to come. "Communism is not like other parties," writes Gurian, "merely an association for particular practical objects or confined to particular departments of life. It possesses a definite and strictly determined philosophy on which it bases its claim to undivided authority. This philosophy is not confined to an isolated sphere of human interest, political, social, or economic but embraces the entire life of man. It is this fact alone which enables it to claim absolute validity and unqualified allegiance. This philosophy, however, is no mere theoretical belief, it is the basis of a solid organization."[1]

Christopher Dawson gives a similar estimate of its nature: "Communism is not simply a form of political organization; it is an economy, a philosophy, and a creed. And its hostility to Christianity is due not to its political form, but to the philosophy that lies behind it. Communism, in fact, challenges Christianity on its own ground by offering to mankind a rival way of salvation. In the words of a Communist poster, 'Jesus promised the people Paradise after death, but Lenin offers them Paradise on earth. . . .' For the first time in the world's history the Kingdom of anti-Christ has acquired political form and social substance and stands over against the Christian Church as a *counter-church* with its own dogmas and its own moral standards, ruled by a centralized hierarchy and inspired by an intense will to world conquest."[2]

The absorption of man into the State is not peculiar to Russia alone; it exists in Russia in an *economic form* where one hundred and seventy millions of God's creatures destined for eternal life are dehumanized and reduced to the state of ants whose sole business in life is to build up wealth for the great anthill of the classless class. It exists in Mexico in an anti-clerical form where it wears a *political* disguise and

----

[1] Waldemar Gurian, *The Future of Bolshevism,* p. 19 (New York: Sheed and Ward).

[2] Christopher Dawson, *Religion and the Modern State,* p. 58 (New York: Sheed and Ward).

identifies treason with worship of the Crucified;[3] it exists to a less degree in Germany in a military form where it wears a *racial* mask, but common to them all is the absorption of the *whole man* into the State, the bludgeoning of men into living their lives without God, and the hammering of man into the pattern of a *homo economicus* with no other destiny than the dust. In each of these countries, and in certain other countries of the world, any attempt to assert the independence of the spiritual in relation to the political, is regarded as counter-revolutionary. The essence of Communism is that God derives His authority from Caesar, and there is no God but Caesar. Regarded from this point of view, Gurian is right in asserting that *fundamentally* there is little difference between the racial "Communism" of Germany and the economic Communism of Russia. "The supremely important fact is overlooked that the methods by which the National Socialists rule the masses are identical with those employed by the Bolsheviks, and must lead to a novel attitude toward the political and social order. A particular political and social order is no longer regarded simply as such, but is made the center of man's entire existence and its claim to that position is supported on philosophic grounds."[4]

How has this world movement of the mobilization of souls for secular ends come upon us? Among other

---

[3] Cf. Wilfrid Parson's *Mexican Martyrdom.*
[4] *Op. cit.,* p. 90.

reasons three may be mentioned: (*a*) Inasmuch as the new philosophy implies the absorption of the whole man into the State, the World War may be alleged as a remote cause, for it accustomed us not only to mobilization, but also to thinking of the relative unimportance of man. When a world which boasts of its progress reaches a point where it can send millions of men *en masse* into a battlefield — it has indeed forgotten that every man has an immortal soul, and in the eyes of God is just as personal and as valuable as the king who declares a war, or the general who directs it behind the lines — indeed more valuable if he loves God more. The inalienable and sacred rights of human personality are indeed regarded as trivial when the bones of six million men can be strewn across the fields for a cause which is still unknown. That war spirit of mobilization which resulted in mass suicide — for that is what the World War was — has left its imprint on the modern mind. The world is still mobilizing, still ignoring the human, still counting bodies instead of souls, still thinking of Poverty instead of the Poor, and of the *masses* instead of man.

(*b*) A second reason, a historical one, also suggests that Communism is not absolutely new; it is new only in the sense that it is last in point of time. In truth, *Communism is the last fruit of a tree that has had its roots hidden for four hundred years in the history of the Western World.* Communism is the last of the three stages in the secularization of the Western World. The first two were: Religious Individualism, and Economic Individualism or Liberalism.[5]

Religious Individualism was begotten of the Reformation which reformed the wrong thing: it reformed faith, when it should have reformed discipline. As a result it eliminated from religion a social, organic body of Truth; namely, the Church, and held that in the domain of religion each individual was free to interpret his own Scriptures; later when Deism eliminated the divine element in the Scriptures, Religious Individualism held that a man's own religious experience was the final court of appeal, and that he could worship at any shrine he saw fit and bow down before the gods his own hands had carved.

The second stage was individualism in politics and economics or Liberalism. In the nineteenth century men argued: If individualism is good in religion, why should it not be good in economics and politics? If an individual is free to decide his own religion without consulting a Church, why should he not be free to decide his own politics and economics without consulting his Bible? If we are to be freed from the

------

[5] The first of these forces contributed to secularism by rejecting the Church; the second by rejecting Christianity; and the third by rejecting the human soul. Consequently if Christian society is going to recover itself, there must be a restoration of these three factors: membership in the Church thrown away by Protestantism, belief in Christ thrown away by Liberalism, and the recognition of a moral conscience thrown away by Communism. Cf. Dawson, *Religion and the Modern State,* p. 148.

authority of Rome, why not also be freed from the
authority of the parson? If the sixteenth century
divorced itself from the Church, why should not the
nineteenth century divorce Economics from Ethics,
Law from Theology, and Politics from Morality? Religion was thus left free to exist alongside the economic
and political order, as two sticks exist side by side.
A man could worship God on Sundays, but the other
six days of the week he could forget Him, for "business
is business." The religious compartment of a man's
brain was never permitted to overflow into his economic or political compartment, though they might
be next to one another. That is why there was a
semblance of morality and an appearance of religion
in Liberalism. It was living on the spiritual capital
of the centuries.

The final stage of the evolution is Communism,
and anyone who knows the logic of history could see
it coming. The Communists argued: If you do not
want religion to influence politics or economics, then
why permit it to exist? If you have eliminated religion from politics and economics, is it not because
civilization has only secular ends? Then why not
consecrate man, body and soul, to the secular? Why
not remake man by unmaking the spiritual? If religion is not permitted to play a part, it must be because
it is a hindrance to the full and perfect development
of the economic order. The ideal, therefore, is the
secular stage in which religion is completely banished

from society. And this is Communism or the philosophy which fills the belly with husks and leaves the soul to starve — the subordination of all values to the economic and all men to the State.

Communism is new, then, only in the sense that a decaying corpse is new in relation to a living man. Communism was not a revolution which began a new epoch; it was a revolution which marked the death of an old one. It is the dying gasp of a civilization which for the past three hundred years has been living without God.[6]

c) A third reason helps also to explain the spread of Communism; namely, the minds of the present day are looking for a complete philosophy of life, or in other words a religion.

Modern man has been uprooted from the past and its traditions; he has moved gradually away from the core and center of his being where his soul is, to the periphery and the circumference which is the superficial, the external, and the material. Politics and economics swallowed him up; the tyranny of wealth, the strife of parties, high-powered propaganda, political injustices and the exploitation of the masses, advertising, and the scheming for power have disgusted him. He is tired of selfish individualism; he is satiated with a democracy that follows the public will, instead of leading it. He feels the need of a reaction; he wants

---

[6] Berdyaev speaks of Communism as the "end of the Renaissance." *The End of Our Time,* Chap. I.

something that will help him return to the center of his being; he wants the spiritual; something about which he can enthuse; he wants something different from anything he has had in the past three hundred years, and since the only Christianity he knows is that emasculated form of it which regards Christ only as man, and which has identified itself with the social order that is passing away, he feels that Christianity has failed, and so the modern man turns to Communism. He seeks it, Dawson says, because it "replaces the doubt and skepticism of an irresponsible indifference, by a certitude of absolute authority embodied in social institution"; he seeks it because he wants a logical system that lays claim to his body and soul. In a word, he is a Communist because it satisfies his need of a religion.

Communism is a religion. This is its positive side. But it is not just a religion in the sense that Humanism is a religion, or even as Confucianism is a religion. If it were only a devotion to an abstraction, like Humanism, or to a vague national ethics, like Confucianism, it would never pull at the heartstrings of man. Communism is not an imitator of heresies; rather it is the *ape* of Christianity itself in its divine and historical form. It has not taken one of the truths of Christianity and emphasized it, as most erroneous forms of Christianity have done in the past three hundred years. Rather it has taken the whole content of Christianity and given it a new soul. It has changed

Christianity in the same way that man would be changed if you robbed him of his immortal soul and gave him the soul of a serpent. The man would see, taste, smell, and generally carry on all the vegetative and animal functions common to the body of man. *Externally* he would even appear as other men, but internally he would be different. Why? Because he would lack a rational soul which is capable of lifting him above the fleeting phenomena of earth to a knowledge and love of the living God.

Communism is like Christianity in its externals.[7] It has its dogmas, its morals, its liturgy, its philosophy of life embracing both body and soul. "Like every other religion, it carries with it an all-embracing relation to life, decides all its fundamental questions, and claims to give a meaning to everything; it takes possession of the soul and calls forth enthusiasm and self-sacrifice. Unlike most political parties, it will not admit secularized politics, divorced from an all-embracing *Weltanschauung*. Its inhuman activity, is, as it were, an explosion of religious energy stored up in the human soul by a lengthy religious process."[8]

Berdyaev rightly says it is not the isolation of a single truth from its organic whole; it is another religion, and the only logical religion outside of historical Christianity; the religion of anti-Christ. A heretic stops

---

[7] Cf. Nicholas Berdyaev, *The End of Our Time*. Essay on the "General Line" of Soviet Philosophy, p. 211 ff.

[8] Nicholas Berdyaev, *The Russian Revolution*, p. 60 (New York: Macmillan).

halfway in his denial of truth; a Communist goes the full distance. It is, therefore, not a heresy within Christianity, but, as was said above, the ape of Christianity; it has its Bible which is *Das Kapital* of Karl Marx; it has its original sin which is class exploitation; it has its chosen people which is the classless Class; it has its Messianic hope which is the world Proletariat; it has its Sermon on the Mount which is its false appeal to the poor and the oppressed; it has its monasticism which is the infiltration of its doctrines through the "cells"; it has its Gospel which is the Gospel of class war; it has its communion of saints which is the comradeship of man; it has its Calvary, which is an appeal to sacrifice oneself for the Communistic state; it has its Kingdom, but without God, the kingdom of the earth, earthly; it lays claim to absolute truth which no politics or economics can claim; it has its catechism which is obligatory on everyone; it has its orthodoxy, and it persecutes its heretics; it lays claim to the very depths of the soul, possessing the conscience and the spirit of man. Only a religion can do this; it persecutes all religions because it claims to be the one true religion and hence can suffer no other; it is the religion of the kingdom of earth, the religion which renders to Caesar even the things that are God's; it is the body of the elect; the new Israel; the ape of Christianity in all externals; it differs only in its soul, for its spirit is the spirit of the serpent.

There is no other explanation for the zeal of Com-

munists than the fact that they accept Communism as
a religion. How else account for the sacrifices it
inspires and the apostles it enkindles? It is so much
a religion, that if it did succeed in tearing out of the
heart of man every spark of Divine Love that is there,
and of uprooting from the mind every quest for the
Eternal Unchanging Truth which is there, and of
crushing every spirit of sacrifice which was inspired
by the Cross of Christ — if it did this, it would make
itself impossible. If Communion destroyed all religion, it would destroy Communism, for it would no
longer find anyone who would have zeal to spread its
truth, or the courage to sacrifice himself for its
propagation. Even the devil would cease to spread
evil, if he did not wear the mask of virtue. Communism is not destroying religion it is only attempting to substitute one religion for another; it is turning the whole world into the Mount of Temptation
where Satan and Christ battle for the souls of men.[9]

---

[9] "Communism is not just an economic doctrine in reaction to Capitalism, though it presents itself as such; it is its logical consummation. The
Spirit of Capitalism contended that the supreme goal of business was
the amassing of wealth, and the increase of production was not for
human needs but to acquire more wealth. The Church was not to
interfere, for business had nothing to do with religion; the State was not
even to interfere, but only to guarantee security and freedom for the
economic machine to function so as to achieve its maximum realization.
Communism steps in and pushes the slavery of man to the economic
order to its logical extreme. The old Capitalism made the economic the
principal basis of civilization. Communism makes it the *unique* basis
of civilization. The old Capitalism wanted no interference from the
State, but left God and religion alone provided they did not interfere.

There is a relative truth, however, in Communism and that is its reaction against Individualism which makes man a wolf to his neighbor; but more than that, its greater relative truth is its longing for a real community of men. Individualism had its day and failed; the social nature of man must be emphasized. But there is not only one kind of unity into which men can be grouped, and that is the mistake Communism makes. There are two: the *organized technical* unity which is Communism, and the *organic spiritual* unity which is Catholicism. In other words, there is a social body in which man is dehumanized for an economic end, but there is also a social body in which the spiritual dignity of man is preserved for eternal happiness with God.

Because Communism does insist on the social and communal, it can never be opposed by any system of ideas, or by any loud shouting about "rugged individualism"; it can be stopped only by something social and communal. Because it mobilizes souls for

------

The new Capitalism or Communism says: if the supreme business of life is to subjugate man to the economic order, to mechanize human life, then why not make the economic order not the end of the individual, but the very end of the State itself? Therefore, no longer entrust the mad pursuit of the secular and the economic to a group of individuals, or a few scattered capitalists. Make the economic the end of everyone. Force it down the throats of everyone; jam it into their souls and suffocate the thought of God; cram it into their hearts and extinguish the fires of Divine Love. The State itself shall be Capitalist. The State itself shall seek Wealth! The Economic shall be the end of man." Cf. A. Fanfani, *Catholicism, Protestantism, and Capitalism,* Chap. II, Essence of Capitalism (New York: Sheed and Ward).

economic ends and crushes the spiritual element in
man, it can only be stopped by some force which
mobilizes souls for eternal ends and preserves the
honor of a man. Because Communism is a philosophy of life, it can be met only by a philosophy of life.
And there are only two complete philosophies of life
available today: the philosophy of Communism which
dehumanizes man to the level of the economic, and
the philosophy of Catholicism which asserts that man
is not only a member of an earthly kingdom, but
is also destined for another world attainable only
through righteous living on this earth. Briefly, there
is no force in the world today which can adequately
oppose Communism except Catholicism, as the Communists themselves admit.

The reason the Church can do it is because
it satisfies the highest aspirations of Communism;
namely, the assertion of the social nature of man,
and at the same time saves man from the great defect
of Communism; namely, the absorption of man into
the State, by asserting that man transcends the State
inasmuch as he is spiritual as well as material.

In order to understand this Catholic Philosophy
of Life opposed to the Communistic Philosophy of
Life, let it be recalled that when it came into being
with the birth of our Lord of the Virgin Mother
over nineteen hundred years ago, the political, economic, and social conditions of the world at that time
were much like our own. For example, in those days

there was an intense Nationalism in Israel, and a
haughty Militarism in Rome. With Caesar there arose
a kind of dictatorship which absorbed individual
rights. Economically, there was exploitation of labor
and the servile state. Taxation was excessive and over-
powering; religion was on the decline; the Gentiles
had lost faith in their gods, and Israel had had no
prophet since the days of Daniel. Wealth was in the
hands of the few; life was becoming more of a riddle,
in which solitary hearts lost nerve, begot no songs and
few children, became weary of old culture, afraid of
new gods, of fate, of the stars above and the world beyond. Vergil, who lived close to those times, described
them as follows:

> Where wrong and right are blest,
> A world that teems with war, a world that reeks
> With countless crime, where evermore the plough
> Lacks its due honor, and the hind is forced
> Far from the desolate fields, and reaping hooks
> Are straightened into swords.

Into this world with its depression, its despair, and
its despondency, God came. And He came to set men
and their world right with God — not only their
hearts and their souls, but even their business, their
secular affairs, their governments, and their all. How
did He do it? God solved the social, political, and
economic problems of the world not by enunciating
a new economic system; nor by instructing man in

the ways of supply and demand; nor by a great piece of research which revealed the many aspects of their problem; nor even by giving to the world a formula for finances, trade agreements, armaments, slavery, imperialism, or war. He saved it from its ills by being born as a babe in the insignificant village of Bethlehem. That seemingly trivial incident which was so commonplace that the innkeeper refused a room to His Blessed Mother was the revolution that upset the world and the solution which gave it peace. Driven even off the face of the earth He came to save, His Mother sought refuge in a shepherd's cave, and there, under the floor of the world, was born Him who like Samson, shook the pillars of the world to its very foundations, pulled down the already crumbling edifice, and built a new Living Temple in its place, where men might once more sing because they had found their God.

But what has the birth of God in the form of a babe to do with the social, political, and economic conditions of His day and our own? What possible relation could exist between a child in a manger of straw and Caesar on this throne of gold? The answer is: *The birth of the Son of God in the flesh was the introduction into the historical world-order of a new life; it was a proclamation to the world that social reconstruction has something to do with spiritual regeneration; that nations can be saved only by the men in them being reborn to God as God is now being born to man.* Once God entered the created order on the level of humanity and became part of the stream of history, He gave man a new strength from above; He gave him a Divine Power along with human power. In a word, God became man in order that man might become Godlike. That is why Christ was born a babe — to teach us that deliverance from economic and social ills can be obtained only by a birth.

Humanity was tired mentally and exhausted spiritually; for thousands of years it had been making the great experiment of Humanism, and was now like a sick man who could not cure himself. It was in a state like unto our own world, which since the days of the Renaissance, has tried to build its civilization on the self-sufficiency of man without God. Mankind, left to itself, slowly sinks downward and reverts to the type of Adam. The law of necessary progress is a myth. We have proof enough that people advanced in culture may degenerate into savages, as our boasted twentieth-century civilization degenerated into the butchery of the World War; but no solitary example exists of a race of savages rising to the civilized state by their own development. Apart from an outside supernatural assistance society goes from bad to worse until deterioration is universal. Not evolution but devolution is the law of man without God, just as it is the law of the sunflower without the sun. With all of our boasted mechanical civilization a day might come when our modern towers of Babel would be as forgotten as the first, when Americans would cease to exist as a race as the Babylonians and Medes have ceased to exist, when Washington would be a contested locality like the capital of the Aztec civilization, and when the Constitution of the United States would be the hopeless search of the world's archeologists. Distant as it may seem, it is something which has happened a hundred times before and which may very well happen again.

Humanity cannot lift itself by its own bootstraps; there is no such thing as spontaneous generation; life does not come from crystals; poetry does not come from donkeys; international peace does not come from wars; social justice does not come from selfishness. With all our knowledge of chemistry we cannot make a human life in our laboratories because we lack the unifying, vivifying principle of a soul which comes only from God. Life is not a push from below; it is a gift from above. It is not the result of the necessary ascent of man, but the loving descent of God. It is not the term of Progress; it is the fruit of the Incarnation. Hence, like that world into which Christ was born, the world today needs not a shuffling of old ideas, not a new economic, not a new monetary system — it needs a new birth. It needs the intrusion into our order of a new life and a new spirit, which God alone can give. We cannot give ourselves this new birth any more than we can be born again

naturally. If we are to be born again into the newness of life the regenerating principle must come from
above, and that is precisely the meaning of the Incarnation: The introduction into the world on the
level of human nature of the Life of God, who came
not to judge the world, but to save it. And this is
why I say He solved our problems by appearing as
a Babe, because the regeneration of society has something to do with birth.

Immediately it is objected: This is but theory; the
Incarnation of the Son of God took place 1900 years
ago, and is just as past as the Battle of Waterloo. No!
The Incarnation is not past. How can God belong
to the past? The Incarnation is taking place *now*.
What God did to that individual human nature
which He took from Mary His Mother is what He
wills to do, in a lesser degree, to every human nature
in the world; namely, to make us partakers of His
Divine Life. He who from all eternity was born of
the Eternal Father was born in time in Bethlehem.
He wills that we who are born in time of our earthly
fathers, should be reborn in eternity of the Heavenly
Father, made new creatures, become possessed of new
life, and members of the Kingdom of God. Let me
make this clear by an example: When a government
wishes to issue a coin, it first of all makes the original
die. This original model requires the work of a con-
summate artist. But once the die is cast, the model
formed, millions and millions of coins may be struck

from it, each bearing the resemblance of the original. Now, Bethlehem is the city where the die was struck and Christ Himself is the die. All the men who have lived and will ever live are the raw material awaiting the stamp of the Divine Original. But in order to be like Him, that is, a sharer of His Divine Life, we must be struck off that die. And all men who are signed by this sign and sealed with the seal and regenerated by the waters of this Spirit from the Church or the Mystical Body of Christ, are the new coins. Religion to Christ, then, was not a purely individual affair, for how could a million men love God without loving one another? Rather did He lay plans to infuse the world with a new society, a new kingdom, a new organism which would be the social prolongation and extension of the Divine Life He brought to earth.

Often during His earthly life, which was not long, as we reckon human life, He promised to assume another body which would be one with Him, as His own physical body was one with His Divine Person. But this new body He said would be *social,* i.e., it would be made up of men, like a kingdom; it would be *vital* and *organic,* i.e., the relation between the new body and Him would be like the relation of the branches and the vine; it would be one with Him, so that if anyone did anything to this new body or new kingdom, they would be doing it to Him; it would be *capable of growth,* i.e., starting with a few chosen apostles it would grow like a tiny mustard seed until it became a great tree and filled the world; it would be both *divine and human,* as He was divine and human, i.e., human in the men who would constitute it, divine in the Spirit which would vivify it. In preparation for this new social existence our Lord gathered about Him a few apostles and disciples, and on Pentecost He accomplished what He had promised; He fulfilled what He had prophesied. He sent His Spirit upon His Church to make it one with Him. Under the unifying flames of that Pentecostal day, Christ began to live socially in His Church as He had lived individually in His human body. As He took a human body from the womb of His Blessed Mother, overshadowed by the Holy Spirit, so now He took His Mystical Body or the Church from the womb of humanity, overshadowed by that same Holy Spirit. And so the historical Christ, who is in heaven at the right hand of the Father, is now living on earth in His Mystical Body the Church, doing the same three things through it which He did with His physical body; namely, teaching because He is Teacher; governing, because He is King; and sanctifying because He is Priest. And that is why we Catholics believe the Church is infallible, why the Pope is supreme, and why her sacraments are holy, because Christ is Teacher; Christ is King; Christ is Priest. Very simply, we have taken Him seriously when He said to His Apostles: "I am with you all days even to the consummation of the world. . . . He that heareth you heareth Me."

The Church, then, is a Body because it is made up of millions of regenerate souls as the body is made up of millions of cells. It is called mystical, because the bond which holds it together is not a vague spirit like "a school spirit," or "patriotism," but rather the Spirit of Love which is the third Person of the Blessed Trinity. As the human body is made of countless cells and organs; as the eye is not the ear, nor the hand the foot, nor the lung the heart, but all parts of one whole, because governed by one head and vivified by one soul, so, too, in the Mystical Body the Church, the nun is not the mother, the priest is not the layman, the missionary is not the cardinal, the altar boy is not the bishop, and yet all are one, because governed by the one head, the Vicar of Christ, and all vivified by the same Spirit which is the Spirit of the Love of God.[10]

Such was the method our Lord chose to regenerate a world: not through a few select individuals, or through an organization of individuals, or even through a communism which would crush personality, but rather by becoming "incarnate" as it were, socially, in a community, in an organism, in a body, or a society which antedates personality and therefore creates it as a child of God.

The Church, therefore, was to be in the world, but not of it; it was to be a *city* set on a hill toward

---

[10] This idea is treated in full by Sheen, *The Mystical Body of Christ.*

which men might turn their eyes to know the secret of their strength, but it was not the hill; it was to be a *light* shining out through the darkness of the troubled world, but it was not the darkness; it was to be a leaven in the dead mass of sin-stained humanity, but it was not the mass; it was to be the *salt* wherewith the earth was to be salted and preserved unto everlasting life, but it was not to be the earth. Above all else it was to be a fellowship based not on the laws of society, or the ties of blood, or the necessities of economics, but on the reordering of the whole field of human relations in a spirit of charity, and the cohesion of shattered and despised humanity under the headship of Christ. And to those who would cry out for the primacy of the economic or political order there was one answer. These things are important; their remedies are available; their problems are solvable, but only on one condition: "Seek ye first the Kingdom of God and His Justice and all these things shall be added unto you."

Such is the philosophy of life of the Church in its most general outline, the details of which have yet to be considered. It is no longer being opposed by heresy, for the days of heresy are over. The future conflict of the world will not be between Religion and Science, or between "rugged individualism" and Socialism, but between a society which is spiritual and a society which is mechanical; between a society which adores God, and a society which claims to be

God; between a society which absorbs man for secular ends, and a society which respects personality and uses the secular as a means to eternal ends. The world must make the choice. The forces are already aligning themselves preparing for a battle. Men will enlist on one side or the other; we must battle either for brotherhood in Christ, or comradeship in anti-Christ.[11] The prodigals will either come back to the Father's house or they will go the way of all flesh and fill their bellies with the economic and the secular. The world of the future will have only two capitals: Moscow and Rome; it will have only two temples, the Red Square and St. Peter's; only two sanctuary lamps, the Red Flag and the red glow of the Eucharistic lamp; only two tabernacles, the Kremlin and Emmanuel; only two hosts, the rotted body of Lenin and the Body of the living Christ; only two hymns, the "International" and the "Panis Angelicus"; but only *one* victory — the victory of Him who has overcome the world.

----

[11] The new order to result from these two camps can be only one of two kinds; either the order whose ruling principle will be the freedom of man subject to God; or the order whose ruling principle will be the freedom of man surrendered to a human despot. There are no other principles of authority. — Ross Hoffman, *Restoration*, pp. 194 ff.

✿✿

Chapter III

THE PRIMACY OF THE SPIRITUAL

THE next scenes in the life of the Prodigal Son reveal the condition of conversion. In a broader way they represent the four conditions upon which the prodigal children of the modern world will come back again to the unity of the Church. The first of these conditions engages our attention in this chapter.

As long as the Prodigal was delighting in the pleasures which his gold and his youth bought for him, there was very little thought of his spiritual destiny. It is a very interesting thing that he did not begin to reflect until he was reduced to dire need and misery. This idea our Blessed Lord expresses in these words: "He entered into himself," which imply that up to this time he was "outside" himself, or "beside himself." All his enjoyments were external to himself: such as food, pleasure, the dance, and in general what some men call "life." In this he was like the beasts of the field, for they seek things outside of themselves. The animal in quest of food, the flower lifting its face to the sun, the bird dipping for the worm — all of these have no other end or purpose in life than some object outside themselves. They can never enter into themselves, for the very simple reason that they have no rational soul. Man is the only being in the world who can reflect, and hence the only one who can turn back upon himself, be angry with himself, be pleased with himself, contemplate his own thoughts, perceive the difference between what he is and what he seems, his own worth and what others attribute to him. He is the only creature in the universe who can look upon himself as in a mirror and see himself as others see him, and even sit, as it were, on another planet and let his feet hang over, contemplating off in the distance a planet which happens to be his very self.

Our Blessed Lord dates the conversion of the Prodigal from the moment when he began to perform the first act of man; namely, to enter into himself. It was that mysterious point at which he ceased to live only for the outside and began to look into his own soul in relation to his needs. He began to contrast the tranquillity of his heart in former days with the bitterness of the passions which succeeded them; he sees now that he was happy only in his early years, and that now his conscience speaks to him only with the universal hiss of sin. He sees, furthermore, that the unity of his moral being was broken, that the senses which should have ministered to reason, and his body which should have served God, revolted and strove to set up empires of their own and make themselves supreme and lords of all they surveyed. He contemplates himself now as a broken vase, and entering into himself tries to piece himself together. It is an experience common to all of us. Even in our own language we use such phrases as "come to one's senses" and "pull one's self together," all of which means inwardness as against outwardness, and the inner life as against the life of dissipation.

The historical application of the parable is this: Civilization will return to sanity and to God only on condition that it "enter into itself"; i.e., it must begin to examine its conscience, and recognize the one thing that makes a man; namely, the spiritual soul.

The great concern facing civilization today is not the problem of unemployment, not finances, not production or consumption, not free trade or world relations or even property rights. The problem of the hour is the *problem of man*. Human dignity is at stake; the value of a human personality is being questioned. Three influences are commonly mentioned as having influenced the dehumanization of man: (1) The machine, (2) Marxism, and (3) false science.

1. There has been much written about the machine[1] as if the machine were wholly bad and should be scrapped. The machine is not an evil;

---

[1] Nicholas Berdyaev, *The Bourgeois Mind,* in his essay entitled "Man and Machine," treats this topic at length.

rather the way it was used produced the evil. A false principle was invoked by Capitalism in the use of the machine; namely, that the primary end of business is production and not consumption. It used the machine not to supply *human needs* (which would have put the emphasis on human dignity), but to increase productivity or wealth for the owner of the machine. Rapid advance in technology enabled the employer to do two things; dispense with human labor, and increase the output of goods. This naturally led to a point where the goods produced far surpassed the capacity to buy. Increased machinery meant increased unemployment, increased unemployment meant decreased purchasing power. The capitalist, then, had to have recourse to artificial stimulation of sales such as advertising, which aroused the buyer into a false sense of need.[2] So magnified did this artificial stimulation become that industry reached a point where it *cost more to sell a product than to produce it.* Such was the logic of a system which conducts a business not on the basis of satisfying a human need, but on the basis of amassing capital as an end in itself. The philosophy behind such a system degraded and depersonalized man by making him only a unit in the production of goods, and only a stimulant to greater production because he was a consumer of goods. Man thus began to exist for

----

[2] Cf. Amintore Fanfani, *Catholicism, Protestantism and Capitalism,* Chap. II, Essence of Capitalism.

economics, instead of economics existing for man. Economic values displaced human values. The "price" was worth more than the man who had not the price. Some even went so far as to advocate the destruction of the produce of nature for the sake of the economic price. Human starvation in the midst of plenty was justified on the ground of economics. Thus, for the first time in the history of the world, man asked Providence to be a little less Providential. "Take back your gifts, O God, for their abundance shatters our economics, even though it does feed the bodies of Thy creatures. Shorten Thy Arm of kindness that the economic price may not perish from the earth."

The logical development of the emphasis on the economic as against the human is Communism, in which man exists only for the economic order, and becomes a tool not of the individual Capitalist but of the Capitalistic State. Man amounts to nothing unless he can produce more wealth for Collectivity. The dignity not only of work, but even of humanity is thus swallowed up in that great anonymity: Communism.[3] That is why it is so difficult to find out who is to blame in the present situation; there is nothing personal one can touch. The world blames the system which is admittedly false. But why is the system false? Because it is anti-personal, because it has violated

---

[3] "Communism teaches and pursues a twofold aim: merciless class warfare and complete abolition of private ownership; and this it does, not in secret and by hidden methods, but openly, frankly, and by every means, even the most violent." — Encycl. *Quadragesimo Anno*.

human dignity; because it has ignored the value of personality. That is why the fundamental problem of the world today is the problem of man.

2. The reaction against Individualism and the emphasis on the mass is the second factor in the depersonalizing of man. Democracy is a very Christian doctrine, the theological basis of which is the brotherhood of men and the Fatherhood of God. Modern democracy became popular just at a time when Western Civilization began to squander its spiritual substance. It became the basis of government at a time when the idea of human personality was divorced from religion, and hence from a sense of spiritual responsibility. Instead of laying the stress on *personality* which is a human and spiritual idea, democracy rather stressed *individuality* which is a material and mechanical concept. A stone is an individual, but not a person. Personality is a spiritual concept involving solidarity; individuality is a physical concept involving juxtaposition. In a democracy where man insisted on his *individual* rights, instead of on his *personal* rights and correlative duties, he was bound to become a wolf to his neighbor. Each one sought his own. Selfishness rather than interest in the organic whole became the law. This selfishness produced extremes of great wealth and great poverty. And then came the reaction.

What one generation of the world believes to be true, the next believes to be false. The pendulum swung away from the extreme of Individualism where each man was a law unto himself, to that other extreme where individuality was submerged in the mass or the collectivity or the State. In the age of Individualism, he was related to his neighbor as a brick to a brick in a house, instead of as a cell to a cell in a living organism, which is the Christian concept. Now he becomes like a drop of water in a glass of wine, dispossessed not only of individuality but of personality as well. Man in Communism has ceased to exist; he is socialized, communized, and dissolved even to the very core of his being. He has no will but the will of the State; no thought but the thought of the Collectivity; no blood but the blood of the race; no rights but the rights of the nation. Mystically submerged body and soul, he no longer has life in God but only life in the collectivity. He has been transubstantiated not into a divinized creature of God, but into a mechanized tool capable of producing the maximum of capital in the minimum of time. Man has ceased to exist; there remains only numbers, instruments, quantity, tools, and all are functions of the mass. There is now no God but Caesar. The older Individualism thought of God as a mental projection of a man, and hence regarded Him as a "human myth." The new Collectivity thinks of God as the mass, and hence as synonymous with society. God is nothing but "society divinized." Psychological Polytheism has given away to Social Pantheism in which God is not the name of a glorified man, but of a deified mass — and this is the last stage in the absorption of all that is fine, noble, and even divine in the creature which was once called man.

3. The final factor responsible for the mechanization of man is a false science which attempts to explain the greater by the less, and feels it has given a complete explanation of anything when it has named its component parts. Psychology, for example, first said that man had no soul, then that he had no mind, and finally no conscience. The truly psychological was explained by the physiological, and man who was once defined as a rational animal was now reduced to the state of a physiological machine which behaved in response to the physical law of action and reaction. Once deprived of his spiritual character and uprooted from the spiritual, as he had been torn up from the great tradition of the ages, this false science now proceeded to mechanize him still more. Biology told him he was the highest thing yet evolved in the universe, and was already on the high road to becoming a god. Physics then proceeded to contradict this view and told him, that in view of the vastness of the universe he was only a "crustal phenomenon" and a mere accident, destined to be dissolved in the great cosmic bonfire. Man thus began to consider himself the world's contradiction; exalted one moment as a god, and the next moment told he came from a beast. Robbed of God by believing He was only a symbol for "the ideal tendency in things"; robbed of will by the "philosophy of events"; robbed of his intellect by theories of knowledge which

doubted his capacity to know; robbed of his soul by the subconscious, the subliminal, and the sexual, he became only an atom dissolved into the mass of a two-dimensional universe of space and time.

The real problem of our day is, therefore, the Forgotten Man; not the forgotten man of a political campaign; not the forgotten man who is unemployed, or hungry or economically dispossessed; not *the* forgotten man, but *forgotten man* — man with a soul, man with a personality, man with duties not only to Caesar but to God, man with a destiny above the mass and the collective in the great brotherhood of the communion of saints where God is love.

The problem of man must be solved first because *it is on his account* that the social problem must be solved. Everything else is ephemeral: economic goods, party politics, finances, and trade agreements pass away. The nature of man is a fixed something like the nature of a triangle, and can no more be distorted by making him a collective atom than a triangle can be distorted into four sides. Unless, therefore, his true nature is recognized, every other solution is bound to fail, if for no other reason than the fact souls are born into the world every minute presenting the same problem for solution all over again. The nature of man is a spiritual and not an economic question. Our political and economic difficulties are merely symptoms of something more seriously wrong; namely, the nature of man and his relation both to his neighbor and to his God.

If social reconstruction is conditioned upon prodigal civilization "entering into itself," which means to recognize the spiritual in man, it now remains to inquire into the nature of the spiritual. This, of course, means saying something about philosophy. To suggest a correct philosophy of life as the solution of economic difficulties may seem to some minds as unrelated as poetry to plumbing. But this is because we have been too accustomed to thinking that action precedes thought, and that practice determines principles. It is just such an inversion of the true order which produces intellectual chameleons who suit the principles to the times, rather than the times to the principles. Even the modern denial of a philosophy of fixed principles asserts such a philosophy, namely, that there must never be any fixed principles. With great justice, Leo XIII wrote: "When a society is perishing, the true advice to give those who would restore it is, to recall it to the principles from which it has sprung; for the purpose and perfection of an association is to aim at and to attain that for which it was formed; and its operation should be put in motion and inspired by the end and object which originally gave it its being. So that to fall away from its primal constitution is disease; to go back to it is recovery."

What are the principles relative to the nature of man which condition the spiritual rebirth of the world? These principles in broad outline are threefold: (1) Man has a final end; (2) Man is a social being; (3) This world is sacramental, or a stepping-stone to the next. Man is a creature set in a triple environment: God, fellow man, and nature; and from these fundamentals all sound economics, politics, and sociology are derived. "For though economic science and moral discipline are guided each by its own principles, in its own sphere, *it is false* that the two orders are so distinct and alien that the former in no way depends on the latter. This so-called law of economics, derived from the nature of earthly goods and from the qualities of the human body and soul, determines what aims are unattainable or attainable in economic matters, and what means are thereby necessary; while reason itself clearly deduces from the nature of things and from the *individual* and *social* character of man, what is the end and object of the whole economic order assigned by God the Creator."[4]

1. *Man has a final end:*

One of the first questions in the penny catechism is: "Why did God make you? God made me to know Him, to love Him, to serve Him in this world and to be happy with Him forever in the next." These words sum up the wisdom of Aristotle and St. Thomas and the best thought of the world both pre-Christian and Christian. It is not faith but reason which concludes that God is the final end of man. Man is neither self-given nor self-created. He therefore must have relation

----

[4] *Quadragesimo Anno.*

not to the secondary cause, but to the Primary Cause who endowed him with being. And since he is a rational creature, these relations of dependence involve the intellect and the will, by which he knows God to be his end and freely chooses to attain Him. As biology cannot exist without life, nor physics without matter, so neither can man exist without God. As the author is entitled to royalties on his book because it is the creation of his mind, so is God entitled to the free and intelligent royalties of man whom He has made.

Now we are in a position to know what is right and what is wrong. Right conduct is that which is natural to man as he really and truly is; not natural for me, or you, or any individual, but to man as he *ought to be.* But man as he ought to be, is a creature destined for eternal union with God. This is not the place to inquire into the basis of ethics, but merely to suggest the principle that morality is related to the final end of man. A pencil is said to be good if it writes, for that is its end and purpose. The action of a man is said to be good if it helps him to attain his end, which is God.

The world thus becomes a stage of character-making wherein all our actions have tremendous consequences. Happiness, like art, is won by effort and struggle and practice. A soul is at stake in the living of a human life for we are not only creatures, but creators of our eternal destiny.

Where, then, find the source of these instincts for life, truth, and love which we already possess? If they are fractions, there must be the integral; if they are reflections there must be the light. Where find the source of light in this room? Not under a chair for there light is mingled with darkness. If I am to find the source of the life and truth and love which is in the world, I must go out to a life that is not mingled with its shadow, death; out to a truth that is not mingled with its shadow, error; and out to a love that is not mingled with its shadow, hate; I must go out beyond time to the Timeless, to Perfect Life, Perfect Truth and Perfect Love that is God. Because God is Life I must serve Him; because He is Truth I must know Him; and because He is Love I must love Him. Hence the true nature of man is a creature made by God, and destined to know, love, and serve Him in this world and be happy with Him in the next. As Oscar Wilde has so well expressed it:

> To drift with every passion; till my soul
> Is a stringed lute on which all winds may play,
> Is it for this that I have given away
> Mine ancient wisdom and austere control?
> Methinks my life is a twice-written scroll,
> Scrawled over, on some boyish holiday,
> With idle pipe, for some song and virelay
> Which do but mar the secret of the whole.
> Surely there was a time I might have trod
> The sun-lit heights, and from life's dissonance
> Struck one sure note to reach the ears of God!
> Is that time gone? Lo, with a little rod,
> I did but touch the honey of romance
> And must I lose a soul's inheritance.

This fundamental concept of rational and moral relations between God and man, involving the eternal
happiness of man with God, permeates the whole of
life. At every moment, from birth to death, man is envisaged as seeking the realization of the "ought to be."
For this end he has been placed here. Hence none of
his actions are insignificant; nothing is indifferent,
nothing is trivial; everything he does, thinks, or chooses
brings him nearer to his goal or away from it. In an
applied sense every economic, political act of man is in
a certain sense a religious and moral act. His final end
is God, and all proximate ends must keep this in mind.
There may be a dozen roads to a certain house but it
is vain to travel any of them if we have not the key.
The means are important and valuable only in relation to the end. "For it is the moral law alone which
commands us to seek in all our conduct our supreme
and final end, and to strive directly in our specific
actions for those ends which nature or rather the
Author of Nature has established for them, duly sub-
ordinating the particular to the general. If this law is
faithfully obeyed, the result will be that *particular
economic aims, whether of society as a body or of individuals,* will be ultimately *linked with the universal
teleological order,* and as a consequence we shall be
led by progressive stages to the final end of all, God
Himself, our highest and lasting good."[5]

Note that the Holy Father judges progress in terms

---

[5] *Quadragesimo Anno.*

of an ultimate end, thus breaking off with the false doctrine of progress which is identical with change. It is nonsense to speak of progress except in relation to a final end, for how do we know we are making progress unless the goal is already fixed?[6] Futurism can never replace ends or purposes or goals. Too often the world has made this mistake, and instead of working toward an ideal, it has changed the ideal, and called it progress. A better word would be "drifting." Once the goal or purpose of life is lost there is nothing left but skepticism and pessimism and a complete conversion to the earthly things which is the sign of mortal sin. It was just such a blindness to the final end of man which has produced our modern cry that "business is business" implying that ethics and morality and religion have nothing to do with business. "Business is *not* business." Business is either good business or bad business, and it is good or bad ultimately because it helps or does not help man to God. Forget the ultimate destiny of man and a new god will be created for him — a cruel god which is the tyrannical State. When Rome

----

[6] "The end of every human act is the glory of God. Man's acts either bring him nearer his goal or further from it. That there be progress every intermediate end must fall in line with the ultimate end. The moral necessity of achieving the final goal circumscribes every activity of man in the political, economic, religious, and every other sphere. Such a conception makes all man's acts, moral acts. Business, study, recreation, work, sleep which can be made a continuous prayer, are the intermediate ends to the final end, God. And this is true progress."— A. Fanfani, *Catholicism, Protestantism and Capitalism,* Chap. V, First Section (New York: Sheed and Ward).

forgot its religion it deified its emperors; when Western Civilization forgets its Christianity, it begins to deify the State.

2. *Man is a social being:*

Man is not only a personal creature with inalienable rights; he is also a social being. In every aspect of his nature, physical, intellectual or moral, man reveals himself as dependent on others. In the society of his fellow creatures man reaches his highest development. Hence he has relations not only to God, but also relations involving family, society, State, nation, and mankind in general. The supreme commandment of love embraces both God and neighbor.

The true doctrine of man as a social being stands midway between the two extremes of Individualism and Communism.[7] Individualism of either the religious type or the economic type which is Liberalism, isolates man from organic relations with his fellow man. Communism, on the contrary, submerges man into the mass. The biological fact that man's physical being consists of a multiplicity of cells, each possessed of a subordinate life of its own, lends the sanction of analogy to a view which treats the entire man as a similar cell in a group life. The golden mean between the extreme errors of Individualism and Communism lies in the doctrine of the *solidarity* of the human race, where personality is real, incommunicable and in-

---

[7] N. Berdyaev, *The Fate of Man in the Modern World,* pp. 76, 77.

alienable, but where it is not self-sufficient either for its own existence or its own fulfillment.[8] The lung must lead its normal life in an organism; to isolate it from the organism, as Individualism would do, is to destroy it; to deny that it has function from a heart or a kidney as Communism would do would kill its individuality. A person cannot come into being except as a member of society of which the family is the basis; on the other hand, society cannot exist apart from the persons who compose it, each striving to attain the highest self-realization.

Christ has elevated this doctrine of solidarity to the supernatural order by extending and prolonging Himself through space and time in His Mystical Body the Church. Our salvation is from the beginning to the end a progressive incorporation into a supernatural society of human souls. The Church is one body, i.e., it is a society of individual baptized souls diverse in function, but moved and vivified by one common life principle or soul, the Holy Spirit. In the human body

----

[8] "Unless it is grasped, the Catholic view of the Church, indeed of society as such, must be unintelligible. We must not get our sociological principles either from Communism, State Socialism, or Individualism. For all these tear the living whole to pieces to exaggerate one portion of it. All are false and diseased. . . . In virtue of his nature man is both an individual person and a member of a society. Nor do these two aspects of his being simply co-exist. On the contrary, society exists already as a living seed in man's individuality, and the latter in turn is necessarily presupposed by society as its foundation, though without prejudice to the relative independence of both these two primary forms of human life." — Romano Guardini, *The Church and the Catholic*, p. 40 (New York: Sheed and Ward).

the soul's action is to a large extent mediated through the head, the seat of its chief organ, the brain, so too the Mystical Body has an invisible head, Christ, and a visible head, Peter, through which the Spirit moves every limb and animates every cell.

There is thus a hierarchy of souls as there are diverse functions of the body. Though every function is indispensable and different they all co-operate harmoniously for the perfection of the body. As the eye cannot say to the ear, "I have no need of your services," neither can a Martha dispense with a Mary nor a missionary with a contemplative. The importance of this doctrine of solidarity for the moral order should now be evident. The ethics is the one law of charity embracing both God and neighbor. No man hates his own flesh, neither should he "circumvent his brother in business" for they are all one in Christ. Pius XI quoting St. Paul's Epistle to the Ephesians makes the Mystical Body of Christ the model of social relations. "If then," he writes, "the members of the social body be thus reformed, and if the true directive principle of social and economic activity be thus re-established, it will be possible to say, in a sense, of this body, what the Apostle said of the Mystical Body of Christ; 'The whole body being compacted and fitly joined together, by whatever joint supplieth, according to the operation in the measure of every part, maketh increase of the body, unto the edifying of itself in charity.' "

3. *The universe is sacramental:*

Man, it was said, is placed in a triple environment of God, society, and nature. It now remains to consider man in his relation to the natural world which has significance because of man's relation to God and his fellow man. The natural world is not evil or something to be fled. It is something sacramental, i.e., it is a material thing to be used for purposes of sanctification, or as a channel for the communication of the spiritual. The natural world is not opaque like a curtain; it is transparent like a window. It reveals God as a building reveals the architect and as a painting reveals the artist. If man were a pure spirit he would have no relation to the world, but being composed of body and soul, he stands as the pontifex or bridge-builder between both. The basic implication of the sacramentalism is that the world is a *means* to an end, and not an end in itself. Matter is a scaffolding up through which souls climb to the kingdom of God, and when the last soul has climbed into it, the scaffolding shall be torn down, for it will have served its purpose of bringing us to God.

Economics and politics are bound to differ widely in proportion as they accept or reject the proposition that this world is a novitiate for the next. A system of economics which begins with the assumption that the world is all, and that future life is an illusion and a snare, will be vastly different from that system which believes it is foolish to spend the day filling our barns

if the Lord that night will require the soul in judgment. "Exclude the idea of futurity," writes Leo XIII,
"and the very notions of what is good and right would
perish; nay, the whole system of the universe would
become a dark and unfathomable mystery." The man
who believes he is one day bound to render an account
of his stewardship will be guided by different economic
principles from those which guide the man who is
worried only about the devils in this world. Deny this
world is sacramental in relation to the next, and you
divorce morals from economics and produce a system
wherein the price of an object is determined not by its
cost of production but by its general estimation; where
the wages of the worker are determined not on the basis
of needs, but on the basis of output; where the whole
energy of man is spent in the improvement of means,
instead of the attainment of a final end; where the
whole of a life is rationalized on an economic basis to
the point of abolishing private property or the family
or even religion, as it is in Russia. There is no escaping
the truth we insisted on from the beginning; the basic
problem of the economic world is a spiritual one: what
is the nature of man? Tell me what you believe about
a man, and I will tell you your economics.

Once the true dignity of man is restored by recognizing that he has a final end; that he is a personality
living his complete life in society with obligations to
his neighbor, and finally, that this world is only a
prelude to the next, then, and only then, can we say
that social reconstruction has begun. As St. Antonius

summed up these propositions: "Production is on account of man and not man on account of production . . . the object of profit is that a man may provide for himself and for others according to their state. The object of providing for himself and others is that they may be enabled to live virtuously. The object of the virtuous life is the attainment of everlasting glory."

If we doubt that our ills are spiritual, let it be recalled that never before in the history of the world has there been so much power and never before have men so prepared to use that power for the destruction of human life; never before has there been so much gold, and never before has there been so much poverty; never before has there been so much wealth, and never before has there been such an economic crisis; never before have there been so many facts, and never before have there been so many unsolved problems; never before has there been so much education, and never before has there been so little coming to the knowledge of truth.[9] It is, therefore, not the material and the

---

[9] "Few can contemplate without a sense of exhilaration the splendid achievements of practical energy and technical skill, which, from the latter part of the seventeenth century, were transforming the face of material civilization. . . . If, however, economic ambitions are good servants, there are bad masters. Harnessed to a social purpose, they will turn the mill and grind the corn. But the question, to what end the wheels revolve, still remains. . . . Economic efficiency is a necessary element in the life of any sane and vigorous society. . . . But to convert efficiency from an instrument into a primary object is to destroy efficiency itself." — R. H. Tawney, *Religion and the Rise of Capitalism*, pp. 282, 283.

economic which has failed us, but the moral and religious inspiration to direct our material resources for the common good and the glory of God. This does not mean that there must not be political and economic and financial solutions; but it does mean these are *secondary*, and that they cannot be ultimately solved until we have "entered into ourselves" and discovered the end and purpose of being a man. This does not mean that anyone who interests himself in these political and economic matters has played false to the Kingdom of God; but it does mean that while due weight must be given the mass legislation as an instrument of reform, these things can be accomplished only by bringing God's breath upon the face of the earth. As Leo XIII states in his *Rerum Novarum:* "If society is to be healed now, *in no other way can it be healed save by a return to Christian life and Christian institutions.* . . . The things of earth cannot be understood or valued right without taking into consideration the life to come, the life that will know no death." In other words, it is the spiritual problem of the nature and destiny of man which conditions all solutions. Pius XI in his *Quadragesimo Anno* adds: "If we examine matters diligently and thoroughly, we shall perceive clearly that this longed-for social reconstruction *must be preceded* by a profound renewal of the Christian spirit, from which multitudes engaged in industry, in every country have unhappily departed. Otherwise, all our endeavors will be futile, and our social edifice will be built, not upon a rock, but upon shifting sand."

The note in both these letters is the same; namely, spiritual and moral regeneration is the condition of political and economic reconstruction. Both economics and politics are doomed to unreality and failure unless grounded on the recognition that man is a spiritual being with ideals beyond this world. To recommend political and economic panaceas for the world problem of dehumanized forgotten man, is like recommending face powder for jaundice, or an alcohol rub for cancer. It is not our bodies that are ill; the soul of civilization is sick. The world is in a state of mortal sin and it needs absolution. Vain platitudes about "regeneration," "the Constitution," and "Progress" are not going to save us, even though we do go on shouting them louder and louder. We need a new word in our vocabulary — and that word is God. We need another standard of judging men than by the wealth they acquire, and that is the virtues they practice. We need less emphasis on the Five-Year Plan and more on the Eternal Plan; for what doth it profit a man if he fill the world with tractors and lose his immortal soul?

Chapter IV

MORE ABOUT THE SPIRITUAL

THUS far the spiritual principles underlying man have been emphasized. It now remains to invert the consideration and inquire into the consequence of civilization's denial of the spiritual. In other words, what will be the consequence of a society organized on a material, secular, and economic basis as contrasted with a society organized on the basis of the spiritual?

In order to understand the consequences of a purely secular culture, the two fundamental differences between matter and spirit must be stressed:

1. *The material is the basis of slavery; the spiritual is the basis of freedom.*

2. *The material is the basis of division; the spiritual is the basis of unity.*

1. *The spiritual is the basis of freedom.* This means that there is no freedom associated with matter. The Principle of Indeterminacy of modern physics is not, as Eddington and Jeans would have us believe, an indication of freedom in nature, but only, as Einstein has told us, a witness to our ignorance of the laws of

nature. Because we cannot tell simultaneously the location and the speed of an electron, it does not follow that the electron is free, but only that we are as yet ignorant. Matter by its very nature is determined to act only one way and not another. Fire, for example, is a slave to heat; water is a slave to seeking its own level; it can never choose to run uphill; ice is a slave to cold. Hence we never praise fire for being hot, nor ice for being cold. They *must* be so; there is no *ought* in their nature.

But once we reach the spiritual, we have freedom. Take, for example, the idea of "house." That idea is spiritual, immaterial, and universal. It has no latitude, nor longitude; no weight or color; it is applicable to all the houses in the world and all the houses there will ever be. Because the architect has such an idea, which is spiritual, he is free to build any type of house he pleases. He can build a bungalow or a castle, a birdhouse or a cathedral. He is not obliged to build any particular kind of house, because no one house completely exhausts that spiritual idea. The spiritual is therefore the basis of freedom.

Another example. An artist has the idea of the "beautiful." That idea is spiritual; it occupies no space or time. No one has ever seen in the concrete, visible, and material world the "Beautiful," though he may have seen a beautiful flower or a beautiful child. Because the idea is spiritual, it follows that an artist is never obliged to paint a beautiful sunset, or a beautiful face, or a beautiful landscape of a beautiful *any-thing,* because no one of these things completely cor-responds and exhausts his spiritual idea of "Beau-tiful." He is free in his art, because the inspiration of his art is the beautiful. The spiritual idea is infinite, but the concrete realizations are finite, and the finite cannot force the infinite, much less than a ten-pound pull can force a ten-ton pedestal from its base.

Because man has a soul as well as a body, he is spir-itual as well as material, and therefore free in many of his activities. It is only where there is Pure Spirit that there is perfect Freedom and that is God. Now to apply this principle to the social order. Assert the spir-itual and you have freedom. Deny the spiritual and assert the primacy of the economic and slavery follows.

The State which acknowledges God in fact and not in mere external profession is necessarily a free State because in *acknowledging God* the State admits that its power over citizens does not belong to it absolutely but has come, as our Lord told Pilate, from God. In other words, a State which genuinely accepts the primacy of the Divine, admits that there are certain rights which man holds *not from the State, but from God; therefore, the State can never take them away.* Therefore, man is free and independent of the State in his right to call (*a*) his soul his own and (*b*) property his own. The Virginia Bill of Rights and the Declaration of Independence emphasize these God-given liberties, asserting that it was "self-evident" that

God had endowed man with "certain inalienable rights."

A man can call his soul his own in a State which acknowledges God, because the *soul* does not belong to the State but to God who made it, and for whom it is destined to return to give an account of its stewardship. Man is, therefore, free to adore God according to the dictates of his conscience, and no power on earth has a right to invade or violate that spiritual sanctuary. To Caesar, he will render the things that are Caesar's, but to God also the things that are God's.

A man can also call a reasonable amount of property his own in a State which acknowledges God, because the right to own private property is not given to man by the State, but by God. Therefore, the State can never take it away. *As the soul is the spiritual guarantee of human liberty, so private property is the economic guarantee of human liberty.* The soul must have a physical expression of its freedom, since man also has a body, and private property is such an expression. When a man owns property, he has responsibility and control which are the attributes of freedom; in times of economic stress and strain, it gives him immunity from collapse. The small landowner in the Alps or France who had only a few acres of land in which he grew the necessities for peaceful existence was, during the depression, more of a free man than he who owned a million shares of stock on margin. A depression can empty half the apartments on Park

Avenue, but it leaves the owner his land. Property is the one certain economic basis of individual independence and freedom of conscience, and this right is a derivative of the spirit; it comes from God. Is it not a confirmation of our thesis that property and freedom go together, to recall that history knows of no instance of a country of well-distributed property ever having suffered from despotism?

The man who lives in a State which acknowledges the Divine above the human, and God above Caesar, is, let it be repeated, a free man, because he has self-determination of his soul and self-determination of his property. In such a State, man is like a mountain whose peak rises above the storms and clouds of the economic and material, where he is free to bathe in the sunshine of God's glorious liberty. The realm of the spiritual becomes a place of freedom and soul relaxation like a home after working hours — an escape from the materialities of an economic world. In brief, as a man's soul has certain powers transcending his body, such as the power of thinking and willing, so man in a religious State has certain inalienable rights and privileges beyond the State, and they are the fountainhead of the greatest liberty of all — the freedom to become a saint.

Now consider the other half of the proposition, viz.:

Matter is the basis of slavery: Apply this principle to a State which acknowledges no God and no soul. Such a State asserts the primacy of the racial, the national, and the economic and is, therefore, a State in which man cannot call his soul his own or his property his own.

A man cannot call his soul his own in such a State because the soul belongs to the State and there is nothing above the State. *On this theory, the rights a man possesses are State given; hence the State can take them away.* If, for example, the right to educate one's family and the right to adore God according to the dictates of one's conscience, are not from God, but from a parliament, then that parliament can dispossess man of these rights. Such a State, which acknowledges no Power above it, always resorts to two kinds of compulsion to destroy the God-given rights of man; first, it forces its citizens by propaganda and fear and oppression, to accept State morality as the only morality and State religion as the only religion; and second, it brands as treason and as "counter-revolutionary" any attempt on the part of a citizen to adore and serve God. If the soul belongs to the State, then it is treason to the State, to dare offer it to God. This is the reason why the Catholic Church is termed "counter-revolutionary" in Mexico and in Russia and Spain. An atheistic State knows full well that it cannot completely possess man as the tool of the State, unless it unmakes the Church which says that man is also a child of God; and that it cannot enslave man until it enslaves the Church which says that man is free. The persecution of the Church in Russia, Mexico, and

Spain is for this reason the strongest proof that the Church is the last bulwark of human liberty left in the world, and the Church is this precisely because she is the last and everlasting defender of the Spirit which makes us free.

Not only does an atheistic State make it impossible for a man to call his soul his own, but also to call his property his own. Since private property is the economic guarantee of human liberty, the atheist State would even dispossess man of that last remnant. The Communistic argument for the dispossession of this human right, is that property has been abused and amassed in the hands of the Capitalists. This is no doubt true, but certainly the solution lies not in the confiscation of all private property, for what is this but to make the State capitalistic? Communism out-capitalists Capitalism by concentrating wealth not in the hands of a few, but in the hands of the State. It then says everyone is rich because the State is rich. Suppose a boy, partly through skill, partly through a larger capital and partly through dishonesty, beats six other boys in a game of marbles. The Christian solution is to equalize the distribution by the introduction of principles of justice; the Communistic solution is to send a big bully into the group of boys to steal all their marbles, leaving them saying: "Now you are all rich, because I am rich, and I am your master."

In an attempt to establish equalitarianism and a classless class, Communism corrects overpossession by dispossession. To use another analogy: Communism finds six men in a row, one wearing diamonds, another not, one wearing a leather jacket, the other wearing evening clothes, one wearing a cap, the other a silk hat. Communism strips them all of their clothes, leaves them naked and says: "Now you are equal! There is no more exploitation! Long live the proletariat." Communism which professed equality on theory has found it impossible in practice. Stalin has even repudiated it. "Every Leninist knows that the leveling of needs and tastes is an absurdity fit only for the *petit bourgeois,* or some primitive sect, not for society organized on Marxist lines, for it is impossible to expect men to have the same needs and tastes and to live under uniform principles."[1]

Stripping private property from man is something like stealing his clothes. It is the deprivation of the symbol of his personality, for private property is the extension of personality. Stealing does not cease to be stealing because the State does it, for "Thou shalt not steal" applies not only to big business but also to a big State. But what interests us at this moment is the fact that the denial of the spiritual and the exaltation of the economic eventually end in the denial of private property. It is indeed an interesting proof of this thesis that the anti-spiritual governments of the world are these which have most denied man the right to call his property his own. Mexico, for example, has denied

---

[1] *Izvestia,* January 27, 1934.

Catholics the right to own property dedicated to the highest of all purposes; Spain has asserted its right to destroy Church property; and Russia, whose first principle is anti-God, has as its second principle anti-private property. At least under Capitalism with all its defects, a few owned private property; under Communism no one owns it but the selfish State.

It is not to the point for the Communist to retort that such dispossession eliminates egoism and solves the problem of justice by equalizing everyone. Such utopianism blinds him to the perennial nature of the social problem. As Richard Niebuhr has pointed out: (1) Social co-operation on a large scale requires some kind of coercion. (2) The instruments of coercion must necessarily be wielded by a particular group who represent the government, such as Communistic oligarchs. (3) The natural force of egoism (which remains inside Communism, though it has become collective instead of individual) tempts these oligarchs to use the instruments of power for their own advantage rather than for the common good. The result is therefore diminished justice, to say the least. (4) The problem is to place the most effective possible inner moral and external social checks upon these centers of social power in society in order to check injustices.[2] It is sheer ignorance of human nature to think that the destruction of private property without religion and

---

[2] "Christian Politics and Communist Religion" in *Christianity and the Social Revolution*, p. 464.

the sanctions of a future life are sufficient to obliterate the manifest traces of original sin and make a paradise of earth. There is a monotony about human nature; and that monotony is principally its weakness and its frailty. Communizing property does not do away with social injustice; it only transfers opportunities for its debasement into fewer hands.

In conclusion, the new slavery is far more serious than the old. The old slavery was only physical. The slave owner did not care how the slave used his soul, or even if he had a soul. He was concerned only with his labor. The new slavery, however, takes hold not only of the body of a man, but also of his soul. It lays hold of the more divine part of him and asserts that he shall not call his property his own, or even his soul his own. He belongs to the State as its draft horse. forced to enrich it as the Communists say the Capitalists forced the proletarians to enrich them.

The Church never tires of pointing to the Cross, where Freedom which is bound up with the Spirit of the Incarnate Son struggled and won over Power, which is bound up with the material and the worldly. With hands and feet nailed to a cross, He who came to give us the glorious liberty of the sons of God was seemingly a slave to the Cross. His enemies asked Him to show His power and come down, but He did not come down, because, if He came down, He would have shown His physical power; He would have *forced* us to do His will; and *that would have been the end of Freedom*. But by hanging on the Cross in an attitude of powerlessness where dug hands could not force obedience, nor pierced feet could pursue the slave, and with only the look of an eye to bid souls reach His side, He preached the lesson of the freedom of man. Even with Almighty Power, He taught that man must be free to love — even God; for by refusing to come down He maintained even in His death, that neither His soul, nor His only "private property" which was His Body, belonged to the State or to Pontius Pilate. His soul was His own, and hence He could give it to His Father; His Body was His own, hence He could give it to us as our Life. He died free, and from that death we derive our liberty. Against the background of Calvary the Church today asserts against the world that no man is satisfied unless he is free, and no man is free until he can love, and no man is free to love until he can love the One for whom he was made; namely, the Christ who loved us enough to die for us that we might be free!

Second Principle: The Material is the basis of division. Matter by its very nature divides and separates men. An apple is material and therefore it can be divided. Suppose it is divided into three pieces. The sharing of the apple becomes a loss for the one who shared it, and immediately creates the question of *my* piece, and *your* piece and *his* piece, and who has the largest piece and why. Or, to take another example, a piece of land is material. Hence it can be divided; one nation wants part of it, another nation wants another part of it. But once divided there is a decrease in the ownership of one and a desire for greater ownership by the other, whence arises quarrels, disputes, and wars.

Spirit is just the contrary to matter. Instead of separating and dividing men, it unites them. Two times two equals four is a spiritual truth, but because every man in the world knows that truth, I am not deprived of the least part of it, as I would be deprived of part of my apple if I shared it with another. In a higher realm, when I receive our Lord in Holy Communion, I do not receive less of Him than my neighbor, nor does my neighbor's communion deprive me in the least of that ineffable gift. On the contrary, the more we share Him the greater our happiness, just as the more we share the truth two times two equals four the greater the unity and the more peaceful our mathematical existences. The Spirit is never diminished by division but matter is.

To apply the principle: The modern world has definitely lost God, and abandoned the spiritual goal of human life. It retains, in some instances, His name but it does not model its life upon His laws, or take any more cognizance of them than it does of the star Betelgeuse. The modern mind has lost its capacity to dwell on the spiritual; it identifies reliance on Providence with the impractical, for its aims are limited by the horizon of time. Like a spoiled child in a nursery it destroys what it has built up, and sulks in the corner amid its ruined toys. It gets itself into a mess by its own selfishness, and then writes a drama ridiculing the idea of God who could make such a world, quite forgetful that God wrote a masterpiece and gave it to us to freely act, and we freely choose to make a botch of it all. To change the simile, the modern world has set fire to its own house, crawls to the roof of it to escape, and then tumbles down amid its ruins, blaming God for not putting out the fire.

Into this mess Russia has stepped to put the alternative clearly before the world: either you will have God or you will have Communism. These are the only two available philosophies left; they are the contradictories between which there is no halfway house, and the choice between them must be determined by what we regard as the end and purpose of life. The choice is between spirit and matter, Church and Communism, God and State tyranny.

But since matter by its very nature divides and separates men, it follows that in a State which exalts the economic, the racial, the political to the end of man there can be no unity either in (a) the economic order or (b) the political order.

a) Economic Order:

If there be no God, if religion be only the opium of the people, if this world be all, and eternity only an illusion; if life be only the dream of the moment and an orgy between two voids; then why should anyone accept his economic lot? Then why should not the poor man who watches the vain parade of diamonds and lace, turn into a robber and a thief? Why should not the rich man seek to exploit the poor man, and throw him on the ash heap of unemployment when the last ounce of energy has been drained from his withered body? Then why in principle should not the lawyers bleed their clients and doctors resort to malpractice; then why should not the bootblack shortchange and the banker swindle, and the maid steal? What answer can be given?

There is only one answer apart from the Spirit and that is, it is the duty of servants to obey. But the thief can answer: "It is my duty to obey only because you are stronger than I, and I can do nothing against you. But suppose I join with millions of other thieves, ditch-diggers, unemployed, and we become stronger than you! Then the role changes. Then it is *your duty to obey.*" And this is precisely what we are witnessing in the economic order today: The law of animality in which the strong devour the weak; and not the law of spirituality where the strong descend to the weak to lift them up unto God.

Take God out of the souls of men, and the more they demand and the less they thank. Take God out of their souls, and the more they stretch out itchy palms to receive, even outriching the rich in their greed. Take God out of their souls and the more they think your hard work and its reward deprives them of their due, even though they do nothing. Take God out of their souls, you take away all restraint upon illegitimate desires, remove all curbs from passions, unchain all concupiscences, and unleash all the furies of selfishness. Then there is no satisfying men. *If this life is all and we are to turn it into a Paradise, then there is no reason why everyone should not have all.*

Once abolish the future life and its influence upon our daily actions, and there is nothing to stand in the way of complete and total equalitarianism. If the only reward is in this world, it immediately follows that all irregularities in rank and condition, all differences in position and office, are open to attack.

b) *The Political Order:*

Note also the loss of unity in the political order as a result of the glorification of the material and the secular and the forgetfulness of the spiritual and the Divine. Just as Communism is an attempt to restore unity to men in the economic order by making them all equally poor and all equally slaves of the State, so dictatorship is an attempt to restore unity to men in the political order. Both these fallacious ways of achieving unity are indications of the discord and division born of a secular civilization. It will be recalled that Liberalism and Individualism of the past three centuries created a selfishness, in which each one sought his own, both in the mental and the economic order. This selfishness reached a point where there was a great amassing of wealth on one side and a great poverty on the other. Man lost his sense of solidarity and social justice and considered himself as isolated from his fellow man, without any obligations to him except philanthropy. There was no longer unity among men, but only a sense of live and let live.

This selfishness needed to be corrected. Unity had to be restored; man must become conscious of the fact that he is a member of society with obligations to the community. But how establish that unity? Religion, which emphasizes the spiritual, could restore it. But men failed to distinguish between ethical and historical Christianity. A new way was hit upon; namely, by an appeal to a dictator. The prevalence of dictators throughout the world is an attempt to achieve unity from the outside to compensate for the loss of unity which religion achieves from the inside. Religion would have united men by love; dictatorship unites them by force.

The unity born of the new era is political, but not spiritual. Dictatorship is based on *power*, but not on *authority*. Authority is personal. Power is impersonal. Our Lord said that the masters of the Gentiles lord it over them, but His authority was personal, because based on His meekness and humility of heart and His love of His Heavenly Father. The dictator's power is based not on his morality, but on his armies, his guns, and his soldiers. That is why in the world today it is difficult to say if there is any such thing as leadership. A robber with a gun is not necessarily a leader because he has a helpless man backed against a wall, nor is a dictator a leader because he relies on his army.

Take a gun away from Hitler, take tanks away from Stalin, and let these men stand on their own moral responsibility with no other power to command than their honesty, their love of truth, and their purity of heart, and see how long they could command. Our Lord has commanded obedience from the world for twenty centuries with no other weapon than a defenseless cross, and the Holy Father has awakened the spiritual obedience of 320,000,000 Catholics scattered throughout the world with no other arms than this spiritual office. But take terror away from Red leaders and they could not command men for four seconds. That is why the new political unity of Communism is not unity; it is compactness through fear, mobilization through arms, nationalization through propaganda, but it is not unity. Remove that fear, those armies, or that propaganda, and these nations would break up into thousands of discordant and warring elements. Only the spiritual is the basis of unity. Take away the religious inspiration and we no longer hear of man helping his fellow man in need, because he sees in him a brother in Christ. With the religious inspiration gone, we hear the need of helping the unemployed only to prevent a revolution. What a sorry commen-

tary on human fellowship! When Christ reigned in
hearts we helped the poor to save our soul; without
religion we help them only to save our hide.

Society cannot long endure under such an inspiration. "Unless the Lord build the house, they labor in
vain that build it." Unity of mankind is lost because
men have lost their God. As a matter of fact, belief in
Christ is the only catholic thing left in the world, the
only bond uniting men in a spiritual fraternity of
love. A Christian in France may differ politically from
a Christian in Germany, and a Christian in America
may differ politically and economically from a fellow
Christian, but they melt all difference in the recognition that God is our end, His Divine Son our Lord
is our Redeemer, and His Holy Spirit is our Sanctifier.
Outside of this, unity is ephemeral, superficial, and
temporary — a unity based on a common mechanical
technique, on a common desire to increase exports
and decrease imports. In some countries, like Mexico
and Russia, the unity is even less; it is based upon a
common hatred of the Church of Christ. Like Pilate
and Herod these nations are one only in their hatred
of a crowned and bleeding Christ.

Thus we come back again to our starting point:
matter divides, spirit unites. The economic as the
end of man is the basis of enmities; the spiritual as
the end of man is the basis of peace.

The world must choose between two symbols, one
the symbol of the spiritual, the other the symbol of

the material; one the symbol of Christianity, the other the symbol of Communism. The symbol of spiritual unity is the Eucharist from which our Lord extends to all men His invitation to eat and drink, that they may be one in Him as He and the Father are one. The other, the symbol of Communism, is the soulless body. When a soul leaves a body, the body begins to disintegrate into a thousand and one conflicting elements which can never be brought to unity again by any process known to man or science. When society loses its soul which is God, it breaks up into millions of conflicting elements which can never be brought into real unity even by force and propaganda any more than dust can be revivified into a living man. That is why I think Communism preserves at the very center of its national life, as the very symbol of its material- ism, and as the rallying point of its revolutionary armies — a corpse — the lifeless, soulless cadaver of Lenin — a perfect symbol indeed of that to which Communism must lead us all — to dust, to dissolution, and to death.

Chapter V

THE BREAD OF THE FATHER'S HOME

THE first condition of the Prodigal's return to the Father's house was the recognition of the spiritual. The Prodigal "entered into himself," that is, he began to do the pre-eminently human thing which differentiates him from the beast; namely, to reflect. The second condition, which we touch on now, is a recognition of a "sense of need." "How many hired servants in my father's house abound with bread, and here I perish with hunger?" The misery, the want, and the spiritual desolation in a foreign land, make him yearn once more to break and eat the bread of the Father's house.

The first condition of the recovery of Western Civilization has already been discussed: it must enter into itself, i.e., respect the true nature of man. The second condition is recognition of its own inadequacy, its own insufficiency, its own hunger, for unless it feels a need how can it yearn for the bread of the Father's house? There is no hope for any civilization which breaks a law and then denies the law; but there is hope for one that breaks a law and still believes in the law. There is hope for a man who is wounded and feels the need of health; there is hope for a man who is deaf and wants to hear, or for a man who is blind and wants to see. But what hope is there for a man who is wounded and says that the wound is good? Or for a man who is blind and does not want to see? Or for a man who is deaf and does not want to hear? Indifference is the last stage of decay, for it leads to that despair wherein man is mastered by fate. Circumstances must not master man; man must master circumstances. This he can do only on condition that he feel the need of something higher and better than the materialities of life which weigh him down.

It may be asked: Does modern civilization feel a hunger for Heavenly Bread? Of this there can be little doubt. Twenty years ago it would have been hardly true to say that the world felt the need of anything. Its prophets had given every assurance that progress was indefinite and that the law of evolution was its necessary guarantee. But that spirit has changed. The cocksureness of everything, even of empirical science, has vanished. There is a general feeling that we are living in apocalyptic times when anything might happen. The World War is now seen in its true light as the objectification of evil, a surface corruption testifying to the unseen cancer eating away the very soul of civilization. Pius XI has summarized the tragic state of the world in his Encyclical *Caritate Christi Com-*

pulsi: "If we pass in review the long and sorrowful sequence of woes, that, as a sad heritage of sin, mark the stages of fallen man's earthly pilgrimage, from the flood on, it would be hard to find spiritual and material distress, so deep, so universal, as that which we are now experiencing; even the greatest scourges that left indelible traces in the lives and memories of people, struck only one nation at a time. Now, on the contrary, the whole of humanity is held so bound by the financial and economic crisis, that the more it struggles, the harder appears the task of loosening its bonds; there is no people, there is no state, no society, no family which in one way or another, directly or indirectly, to a greater or lesser extent, does not feel the repercussion. Even those very few in number, who appear to have in their hands, together with economic wealth, the destinies of the world, and who with their speculations were and are in great part the cause of such woe, are themselves quite often the first and most notorious victims, dragging down with themselves into the abyss, the fortunes of countless others, thus verifying in a terrible manner and before the whole world what the Holy Ghost has already proclaimed for every sinner in particular: 'By what things a man sinneth by the same also is he tormented.'"

Fortunately, there is in the midst of this "confusion worse confounded" a feeling of need, a homesickness for peace, a yearning for the bread of the Father's house. This is proven not only by the willingness to grasp at any solution to lift us from the depths, but even by the growth of Communism itself, for the appeal of Communism is the appeal of a philosophy of life; something which makes claims, inspires sacrifice, and demands everything in the life of man.

The purpose of this chapter is to discuss the applications of one of the most spiritual truths in Christianity; namely, the Eucharist, to the problems of the day, and to suggest that man lives not by the bread of the body alone, but also by the Bread of the Father's house which nourishes unto life everlasting. The Eucharist is chosen because it reveals with unique emphasis the true nature of man, and as it has been indicated before that is the problem of our times. It further suggests that the most spiritual truths in the Church have tremendous ramifications even in the economic and political order.

The world has speculated often concerning the secret of the unity of the Father's House during 1900 years, and has generally attributed this unity to its organization. But that is not the answer. The source of the unity of the Mystical Body is not only the Holy Spirit, who is the soul of that Body, making all one in Christ, as the human soul makes all the parts of the body one; it is not only the Vicar of Christ, its head, who makes that body conscious of its visible unity as my head is the seat of the consciousness of my organic life. The secret of its unity is also that it is nourished by the Divine Life of Christ which is the Eucharist.

An example will make this clear. Some years ago a Russian botanist by the name of Timiriazeff planted a willow wand weighing five pounds in a pot containing 200 pounds of soil. He observed this willow for five years, and at the end of that time took it out, removed every grain of adhering soil, and found that the tree which originally weighed five pounds now weighed 169 pounds and 3 ounces. But so little had been drained from the soil that when it was weighed it was found to have lost only ounces of the original 200 pounds.

Where did the 164 pounds and 1 ounce of increase in the weight of the tree come from? It was not principally from anything visible or concrete. It came in great part through the leaves which were in communion with the great invisible world of solar energy. Now, in the Church something of this kind takes place. The Mystical Body has grown from a tiny mustard seed into a great living Tree of Life. Its increase, however, is not due to the human elements which compose it, for God knows, it would long ago have tumbled to ruins. It came from the communion of the faithful with the Eucharistic Christ. What the sun is to the leaf, that, and infinitely more the Eucharist is to the individual soul. Each Catholic is a leaf on this great Tree of Life reaching out to the Invisible Reservoirs of Life and Love, which is the Eucharist, drawing into himself and into the Body of which he is a member, the strength of Him who has overcome the World. That is why the Church is immortal. That is why her enemies can never kill her! She is nourished and sustained by the immortal Life of Christ!

Let it not be thought that such a spiritual doctrine as the Eucharist has no relation whatever to the problem of our day. If we have any such suspicion, it is only a revelation of how far we have lost the sense of the sovereignty of God in human history. In order to show its application to our day, contrast the triple superiority of the Eucharistic over the Communistic Philosophy of Life. The Eucharist alone recognizes (1) the value of a man, which Communism despises; (2) the Eucharist emphasizes the primacy of brotherhood over equality which Communism falsely exalts, and (3) the Eucharist makes sacrifice and not class struggle the inspiration of battle.

1. The first great advantage of the Eucharistic Life over the Communistic is the value it sets upon a man. Capitalism considered every man a "hand," and hence employers were wont to speak of having ten thousand hands in their factory: the newer capitalism of Communism considers every man a "stomach," something to be fed like a beast of the fields as long as he works to amass wealth for the great capitalistic State. The Church, on the contrary, says man is neither a hand nor a stomach, but a creature composed of body and soul, made unto the image and likeness of God, and destined one day like the planets to complete his orbit and return unto that same God of Love who made

him. The Church has ever insisted that mobilization must not minimize the value of a soul, and that collectivity does not make even a single soul less precious. Millions may go to war wearing only a tag, hundreds of thousands may go into factories with only a number, or may swell the breadlines under the generic title of the unemployed, but for the Church each of these souls is just as precious in the sight of God as the soul of a Shakespeare or a Washington. And why is each man precious? Because God loves him, and loves him so much that He paid an infinite price for man; namely, the Blood of the Lamb slain from the beginning of the world. A man is worth something not only because the God-man died for him, but also because He lived again for him, nourishing him like a mother nourishes her babe, with His own everlasting life. However low he may sink, man is still an exile from the royal household of God for the King has issued the command: "Go out quickly into the streets and lanes of the city, and bring in hither the poor and the feeble and the blind and the lame." Or to paraphrase it: Call in the hungry tramps, the beggars sleeping under papers on park benches, the sandwich men placarding on their broken frames the latest luxuries, the sidewalk artists awaiting the drop of a penny, the half-nourished bodies who crowd the outpatient wards of hospitals, the offscouring of the earth, the broken earthenware of humanity, call them in, all of them; and these same souls who a moment before would have thought a breadline a Paradise, and who would have picked a crust of bread from the gutter, call them in, tell them they have an immortal soul, sit them down at the Banquet of the King and nourish their souls with the Bread and the Life and the Wine that germinates virgins. Judge them not by the clothes they wear, their accent, or their knowledge of world affairs. Give them Divine Life, for their souls have need of life as well as their bodies. Tell them they are not just men, but children of God; infuse their peasant blood with the Blood of Royalty; rejuvenate their hungry bodies with the Meat which nourishes unto life everlasting; lift them up from the slavery and serfdom of the world to the aristocracy of the family of the Trinity; let them forget for the moment their relation to the State, to the family, to society. Let each soul stand naked, face to face with God in a private audience with Divinity, where spirit meets spirit, so that each may rise from the tryst as a new creature, conscious that he must be worth something since God loves him so!

Which of these two views of man is nobler; the one which regards him as a biological entity no more than six feet tall, apt to be killed by a stroke of lightning or the fall of a tile from a roof, standing self-poised and self-centered in such a universe as this, with the finer aspirations of his soul shriveled and dried, acknowledging no God except the State which crushes his soul and absorbs his conscience; or, that same being conscious of his own actual sinfulness, his own possible sanctity; his own actual earthliness, his own possible heavenliness; and then by an act of sacrifice which is the highest kind of daring, surrendering himself to his Lord and Maker at the Eucharistic rail, and crying out in the ecstasy of joy; "I am Thine, O Lord, help me whom Thou hast made." If the latter is the nobler view of man then the Eucharistic Manifesto says to those who would pervert the nature of man: "Communists, you have nothing to lose, but your chains."

2. The Eucharist not only sets a value on man by making it possible for him to commune with God, but it also makes it possible for man to commune with his fellow man. The first effect of the Eucharist is personal; the second effect is communal and social, inasmuch as the soul is introduced not only to its Maker, but to his brother, in that fellowship of the saints, and organized society of spiritual units where the integrating principle is Love. The point here is to suggest how the Eucharist is the Bond of Fellowship. An example will make it clear: What the blood plasma is to the human body, that the Eucharist is to the Mystical Body. In the human body is a lymph flowing through the bloodstream, carrying a store of provisions which is tapped by each individual cell; supplying it not only with the food it needs, but also repairing its waste parts. This flowing tide of sustenance passes by every door, displaying and offering its goods to its tiny little

cells, making them all one body because all are nourished by the same food.

The Eucharist is the lymph of the Mystical Body.
Like a mighty river it swells and sweeps through the
Church in every part of the world, breaking its secret
of salvation to every individual Catholic, whispering
its wonderful message of love for the healing of
wounds to this one, dipping the chalice of its wine
for the increase of joy to that one, thus making them
all one because nourished by the same Bread. Such is
the meaning of the words of St. Paul: "All who eat
the one Bread are one Body." This is the Christian
foundation for the social order, for international
peace, for brotherly love — unity in Christ Jesus, our
Lord.

What is the value of the Eucharistic fellowship over
Soviet comradeship? Recall the three words which
have rung around the world since the French Revolution and which are still to be dimly seen inscribed on
the public buildings of France: "Liberty, Equality,
and Fraternity." Which of these is first? With which
shall the social order begin? Liberalism said start with
"Liberty" — let a man be free to amass wealth without
any interference either from the State or religion.
Liberalism had its liberty, which was only another
word for selfishness, and it brought neither Equality
nor Fraternity. Communism, only different in name,
starts with Equality or the development of a homo-
geneous jellylike state in which all men were equal

because all servants of the capitalistic state. They have had their equality, God knows, which was another name for tyranny, and it destroyed both Liberty and Fraternity. The Church says both are wrong.[1]

----

[1] "Then only will it be possible to unite all in harmonious striving for the common good, when all sections of society have the intimate conviction that they are members of a single family and children of the same Heavenly Father, and further that they are, 'one body in Christ and everyone members one of another.' Then the rich and others in power will change their former negligence of their poorer brethren into solicitous and effective regard; will listen with kindly feeling to their just complaints, and will readily forgive them the faults and mistakes they possibly make." — Encycl. *Quadragesimo Anno.*

The Church condemns absolute equality which denies the very idea of status, and looks upon society as a collection of identical units. The communist attempts the impossible thing; he would make men equal, but succeeds only in ruining men by leaving them at the mercy of economic forces, for the communist judges man by what he has, and not by what he *is*. Against this, the Church maintains that the organic conception of society involves two principles: (1) hierarchy and authority; (2) mutual dependence and responsibility between its members.

In his later Encyclical, *Rerum Novarum,* His Holiness in strong terms writes: "Let it be laid down, in the first place, that humanity must remain as it is. It is impossible to reduce human society to a level . . . all striving against nature is vain. There naturally exists among mankind innumerable differences of the most important kind; people differ in capability, in diligence, in health, and in strength; and unequal fortune is a necessary result of inequality in condition."

As for the censure of the so-called modern liberties we refer the reader to Pope Leo XIII's Encyclical *Immortale Dei.* For natural and moral liberty we can get the Church's teaching at length by the same Holy Father in his Encyclical on *Human Liberty.* If men were to grasp the true meaning of liberty, such as reason and reasoning can explain, they would not assert that the Church is the enemy to individual and public liberty. "The nature of human liberty, however it be considered, whether in individuals or in society, whether in those who command or in those who obey, supposes the necessity of obedience to some supreme and eternal law, which is no other than the authority of God, commanding good and forbidding evil."

She says you cannot start with either Liberty or Equality; you must start with Fraternity or Brotherhood. Brothers may share, but sharing does not make them brothers. That is the mistake of Communism. Thieves may share their loot, but such equality is only the equality of gangdom and not a brotherhood. The workers in a tractor factory in Russia and the Communist spy systems are equal in the eyes of the State where there are no classes, but it is ridiculous to say they are brotherly.

There is only one way to build up a social order where men are free and equal, and that is by starting with brotherhood. But there is only one way in the world to make men brothers, and that is by giving them a common body and a common blood. And there is only one Father in the universe who is good enough and infinite enough to make us all His adopted sons, and that is the Heavenly Father who so loved the world that He sent His Beloved Son into the world to give us His Body and His Blood.

Thanks to the Eucharist, the age-long symbol of the common meal becomes the basis of the brotherhood of men and the Fatherhood of God. Just as many grains of wheat make one bread, and as many grapes of the vine make one wine, so we who are many are all made one in that Bread which is the Body and that Wine which is the Blood. Once men are made brothers of Christ and sons of the Heavenly Father at the communion rail, they are both equal and free: *equal* be-

cause God loves each infinitely, and because each has
a common need which God alone can supply; *free* because each soul is one with Christ, who can do all
things that are good, and what greater freedom is
there than this? The Communists want a classless class.
So does our Lord: "For one is your master and all
you are brethren." But this unity is achieved not by
snuffing out the personality of a man for the sake of
the State, but by realizing its perfection in the God
for whom he was made. The Communion rail is, for
that reason, the greatest democratic institution on the
face of the earth. It is an even greater leveler than
death, for there the distinction between the rich and
poor, the learned and unlearned disappears; there the
millionaire must take the paten from the common
laborer, the employer must kneel at the same board
as the employee, the university professor must eat the
same bread as the simple woman who knows only how
to tell her beads.[2] The dividing wall between national-

---

[2] "The same idea has been expressed by St. Paul when he wrote: *For
we, being many, are one bread, one body, all that partake of the one
bread* (Cor. X, 17). Very beautiful and joyful, too, is the spectacle of
Christian brotherhood and social equality which is afforded when men
of all conditions . . . gather round the holy altar, all sharing alike in
this heavenly banquet. And if in the records of the Church it is
deservedly reckoned to the special credit of its first ages that *the multitudes of the believers had but one heart and one soul* (Acts IV, 32)
there can be *no* shadow of doubt that this immense blessing was due
to their frequent meeting at the divine table; for we find it recorded
of them: *They were persevering in the doctrine of the apostles and in
the communion of the breaking of the bread* (Acts II, 42)." — Encycl.
Mirae Caritatis.

ities is broken down and rebuilt into that spiritual
Kingdom where all are one, because there is one Lord,
one faith, one baptism, one bread. Every prayer is
said in the great context of that brotherhood where
every selfish act to the rich and every envious deed of
the poor is envisaged as a hindrance to the unity of
that Body. It follows, then, that the way to be a real
Communist is to be a Communicant and bring one's
heart to the anvil of Divine Life and have it forged by
the Eucharistic Flames of the Sacred Heart, into that
unity where we call one another not the atomic name
of Comrade, but the spiritual name of Brother.

3. Finally, the Eucharist makes sacrifice the inspiration of victory. Here we touch on another common
aim of both Church and Communism; namely,
violence. Communism achieves its victory by violence;
So does Christianity. "The kingdom of heaven
suffereth violence and only the violent shall bear it
away." But what a difference The violence of the
Communist is toward *his neighbor;* the violence of
the Catholic is toward *himself.* The violence of Communism is class struggle, mutual antagonism, fear,
sabotage, hatred, and malice. According to Communistic morals any violence is justifiable so long as it
redounds to the proletariat state. The violence of the
Catholic, on the contrary, is against himself, or a
struggle against his lower passions, his baser concupiscences, his hatred, his selfishness, his egotism, his
envy, in a word anything which would stand in the

way of pouring out his soul in love both to God and neighbor. He is bidden to go so far in violence to himself that: "If thy hand scandalize thee, cut it off, for it is better to go into everlasting life maimed than to lose one's soul." But he is forbidden to cut off the hand of his neighbor. Lunarcharski, the Soviet Commissar of Education, has well expressed the difference: "We hate Christianity and Christians. They preach the love of neighbors and mercy, which is contrary to our principles. Christian love is an obstacle to the development of the Revolution. We must learn how to hate, and it is only then we shall conquer the world." But hate is not our law, as our Lord told us: "You know that they who seem to rule over the Gentiles lord it over them; and their princes have power over them. But it is not so among you: but whosoever will be the greater shall be your minister." They say we must learn to hate; we say that we must learn to love, and the only way to show love for God or neighbor is by the sacrifice of egotism and by making our dead selves a steppingstone to higher things. Love does not mean, to own, to possess; it means to be owned, to be possessed.

Here we touch upon the sublimest note in the Eucharist; namely, the Eucharist as a *sacrifice*. The end and purpose of all Christian sacrifice, we have said, is to extend not the proletariat state but the Kingdom of God on earth. But these individual sacrifices of ours must not be isolated and haphazard for the Kingdom

of God is social. Our sacrifice, therefore, must needs
take on a corporate or social form. To this end the
Church gathers up our fragmentary sacrifices, harvests
them, coalesces them, collects and masses them, and
unites them with that one great Sacrifice which is
the inspiration of all sacrifice: the Sacrifice of Him
who poured out from the chalice of His Sacred Body
the Blood of the world's Redemption; and this union
of *our corporate sacrifices with His Sacrifice is the
Mass*. The Mass, then, is the sacrifice of the Mystical
Body of Christ, the corporate Calvary of the world,
the social Cross of the Universe, wherein human lives,
escaping the thralldom of the economic and the servi-
tude of the earthly, come to that tremendous and
awful Reality with their tiny crosses and offer them
up in union with the Great Cross of Christ for the
salvation of the world. And then during those most
solemn moments of history, the moment of the cele-
bration of a Mass when the infinite enfolds the finite,
the Eternal breaks into time, and the spiritual clothes
itself with the material, we witness the unfolding of
the three acts in the drama of the Prolonged Calvary.
In the first act, the Offertory, we offer our sacrifices to
Christ under the symbols of bread and wine for just
as wheat becomes bread only on condition that it pass
through the Calvary of a mill, and just as grapes become wine only on condition that they pass through
the Gethsemane of a winepress, so too we become fit
offerings for Christ on the altar, only after we have
done violence to our selfishness and brought ourselves

and the fruits of our honest human toil and labor to the altar to be sanctified unto God.

Then in the second act of that drama, which is the Consecration, we ask God to take us and our poor human efforts and sacrifices, our tears and sorrows, which we have offered to Him under the symbols of bread and wine and transubstantiate us into new creatures of God, saying unto Him: "This is My Body; This is My Blood. Take it, and all that goes with it. Take it as Thine; transubstantiate me, so that like bread, and wine I may no longer live unto myself, but unto Thee; let the accidents and species of my life remain, for they matter little— my name, my appearance, my vocation in life, my routine duties — *but my substance,* change and transform it so that it is no longer mine, but Thine; so that when I walk again with men, they may say to me as the maidservant said to Peter: 'Thy speech doth discover thee.' Thou hast been with the Galilean."[3]

Finally, in the last act, the Communion, the human nature which we offered to Him, and which has now been transubstantiated into a God-surrendered and God-centered life, completes its rhythm. Love reaches its peak not in the unity of the flesh, but of the Spirit, when our Lord says to us: "You give Me your time, and I will give you My Eternity; you give Me your humanity, and I will give you My Divinity; you give Me your death, and I will give you My life; you give

----

[3] Cf. Sheen, *Calvary and the Mass.*

Me your cross, and I will give you My Crown; you give Me your nothingness, and I will give you *My all.*"

The real way, then, to establish the classless class is not by hatred and class struggle, but by love and communion. Men are not called to be pessimists shouting and shrieking that life is too short, because it does not give a man a chance to finish his Five-Year Plan; they are called to be optimists rejoicing that life is long enough to complete their Eternal Plan. Souls are not so many sticks to be thrown into the great cosmic bonfire to keep it blazing for the next generation; each one is a living stone to be cut from the great quarry of humanity, and then squared and fitted into the Temple of God, by the Hand of the Heavenly Architect whose name is Love.

Is the Eucharist, as a solution for world troubles, too idealistic? Is it to be condemned because it is impractical? When a machine is half out of order any tinker can fix it, but when it has gone radically wrong you need something more than a practical man. And so it is with the world today. It is too far gone for practical solutions. There is only one way left to effect social and economic reconstruction, and that is by spiritual and moral regeneration through the Eucharist and the Sacrifice of the Mass.

In his Encyclical, *Mirae Caritatis,* Pope Leo XIII stresses at length the Eucharist and the Holy Sacrifice as the salvation for men who banish God not only from civil society, but from every form of human society. He writes: "History bears witness that the virtues of the Christian life have flourished best wherever and whenever the frequent reception of the Eucharist has most prevailed. . . . It is not too much to say that a great part of the human race seems to be calling down upon itself the anger of heaven; though indeed the crop of evils which has grown up here on earth is already ripening to a just judgment. Here, then, is a motive whereby the faithful may be stirred to a devout and earnest endeavor to appease God the avenger of sin, and to win from Him the help which is so needful in these calamitous times. And they should see that such blessings are to be sought principally by means of this Sacrifice."

Our Lord chose to redeem and transform the world in an extremely impractical way. Extremely impractical it was to put down economical and political injustices by dying on a cross; impractical indeed it was to win a victory over the hardened hearts of men by going down to defeat; impractical it was to save a selfish world by the Love which ended in the Sacrifice of the Cross. No wonder the practical-minded men and women of His day came beneath the Cross and challenged Him to come down. "Come down from Your Cross of impracticality. Come down and shake dice for the garments of God. Come down from Your cross of Love to our class struggle and our hate. Come down from Your love of God to a love of Caesar. The only man who will ever save us is the practical man, who has 'both feet on the ground.' But You have not both feet on the ground. You are suspended between heaven and earth, rejected by the one and abandoned by the other." But He did not come down. And why? Because it is practical to come down; because it is human to come down; because if He came down He never would have saved us! But it is Divine to be impractical; it is Divine to hang there!

Chapter VI

THE AUTHORITY OF THE FATHER'S HOUSE

THUS far we have considered the two conditions
of the Prodigal's return; namely, entering into
himself or recognizing the primacy of the Spiritual,
and second, admitting a sense of need or a yearning
for the Bread of the Father's House. We now come to
the third condition: the recognition of authority. In
the words of our Lord, the Prodigal then said: "I will
arise and will go to my Father." These words are important, but equally important are the words which
the Prodigal left unsaid. There are three things which
he *did not say.*

The Prodigal did not say: "I will search for other
prodigals who are in the same impoverished condition as I, and I will ask them to join with me, and
form a union of all those who have left their father's
house. The group we shall call the 'Federation of
Prodigal Children.' "

Secondly, the Prodigal did not say: "I will make a
philosophy to suit my fallen condition. I shall teach
that morality and virtue are only fictions, and that the

acids of modernity have eaten away the moral beliefs of my father. Hence we need a new authority and a new morals to suit the new age in which we live."

Finally, the Prodigal did not say: "I will go back to my father's house on condition that he sacrifice a few principles of his authority, and that he admit there are other ways of being a son than by acknowledging him to be a father, or else that he permit me to continue some of my old habits even while living within his house."

The Prodigal said *none of these things.* He made no conditions, pleaded no case, asked for no compromises. What he did say was: "How many servants in my father's house abound with bread, and I perish here with hunger? I will arise and will go to my father." What do these words imply? If language means anything, they meant the complete, full, and unqualified acceptance of the Father's authority as the only pathway to real liberty and freedom.

He cared not how humiliating the return might be; he did not speculate as to how arduous would be the journey, or how stony would be the path; his heart was filled with only one thought: "I will arise and will go to my father. He *is* my father, and I am his son."

In the interpretation of this parable, Western Civilization is the Prodigal Son who asked the spiritual Father of Christendom for its share of the substance: the spiritual capital garnered through the centuries, truths, like belief in the divinity of Christ, the existence of God, and the necessity of religion. Western Civilization then proceeded to dissipate and spend that capital. We now pass on to the new condition which has reference to religion, viz.: If there is to be a revitalization of the religion of Western Civilization, it must be accomplished in exactly the same way as the Prodigal himself returned; namely, by recognizing the authority of the Father's house. If there were any other way, our Lord would have indicated it. The religion of Western Civilization certainly is not going to recover its heritage if it insists on saying the things which the Prodigal did not say.

a) It will not regain its heritage by saying: "I will go and find other children like myself who have left the Father's house. I will seek a union among those who have broken with the authority of the spiritual father, and I will call it a federation of churches." Amputated arms and legs cannot enter into conference and give themselves life; the only condition upon which they can live is by being grafted on to the body from which they were cut off. The union of churches will never be effected by denying parentage, but only by seeking it; not by repudiating the Father, but by accepting him; not by throwing away the map, but by picking it up and following all the roads and highways back again to that eternal city where rises the dome of the Father's house.[1]

---

[1] In his essay on "The Road to Freedom," Romano Guardini shows the undeniable relation between freedom and authority. See his work: *The Church and the Catholic,* pp. 67–91.

b) The unity of Christendom will not be effected by the prodigal children saying among themselves: "Let us, like other Walter Lippmans, write a *Preface to Morals* and claim that men cannot live according to traditional morality, that the 'acids of modernity' have eaten away traditional beliefs, and that we need a new ethics to suit our unethical lives and a new morals to suit unmoral ways of living." Such was not the solution of the Prodigal, and such cannot be the solution of the prodigals. The fallacy of such a solution is that it assumes that what has happened is for the best, and that because modern civilization has wasted its substance, therefore it must make a philosophy suited to that condition. It also assumes that men must think the way they live instead of living the way they think. If a number of motorists broke the traffic laws, would we say that the acids of modernity had eaten away the law, and that we should write a *Preface to Traffic Laws;* or would we insist on motorists obeying the traffic law? Would not the crisis be not in the law, but in the lawbreakers? If an epidemic arose in a land, would we say that since people are no longer living according to the laws of hygiene therefore we must revise our hygienic laws to embrace disease, or would we crush the epidemic and retain our faith in health and cleanliness? In like manner, the proper way to heal the ills of civilization is not to suit ethics to unethical lives, but to restore obedience to the moral law of God."

Why should prodigals complain about the exclusiveness of the Church? Do they not forget that each of us can have only one Father, though we may have a dozen stepfathers? While it is perfectly true to say that God distributes His blessings to all mankind, it does not follow that no one has been especially commissioned to dispense those blessings. Mercies given to multitudes are nonetheless mercies because they are made to flow from particular sources. Indeed, practically all of the great appointments of Divine Goodness are marked by this very character of what men call exclusiveness; God distributes all of His gifts to men, but through very select instruments: wealth, power, knowledge, science, art — all of these tend to the welfare of a community, and yet for all that, they are not given to all, but are channeled out to the all through a few. There is a tremendous amount of exclusiveness in the way Almighty God has dispensed the secrets of nature to us. Why should we complain about the exclusiveness of the Church as the channel of divine goodness, when there is far more exclusiveness in the Einsteinian theory of relativity? The great works of art which adorn our homes have come to us from very few artists, and great literature comes to us from perhaps no more than a few dozen authors. The light and heat which nourishes the earth is not supplied to each individual plant and flower, animal and man, by an individual sun; there is only one sun to light the world.

Furthermore, it must be remembered that the exclusiveness of the Church is a condition of membership. Every club, organization, and institution is exclusive in the sense that those who join them must submit to their conditions. If the members of the separated churches feel this exclusiveness, they must be reminded that it is they who created the painful situation. Exclusiveness serves one good purpose: it does not allow the divisions of Christianity to be skimmed over, but keeps alive the need for closer union among Christians even to the point of painful pressure.

It is not at all to the point to say: "There are many roads leading to the City Hall, and yet they all end there. So, too, there are many ways leading to God, and it makes no difference which road we travel." That solution would be all very well if our Blessed Lord had ever said that entering the Kingdom of Heaven was like traveling down a road. Even though it were, it would be a question of taking the road He wanted us to take, rather than the road we wanted to take. But it is not a question of a road taking us to the Kingdom of Heaven, but a key; and there is one very peculiar property of a key, which is that it fits only one lock, and the key of Heaven is hanging from the cincture of the Fisherman Peter. All the present-day appeals for Church Unity are based on the denial of absolute truth and the assumption that unity can be achieved by sacrificing immutable principles. The

Church declares there is no unity possible except by return to her Sacraments and her Authority. The difference between the two views can be illustrated as follows: Suppose there was a convention of mathematicians: one mathematician contended that two and two make three, another that two and two make six, another that two and two make nine. Finally, to bring order into the chaos, it was decided to compromise, and they agreed among themselves that two and two make six and a half. All the while, there is a group of mathematicians who protest and contend that two and two are four. The retort given to them by the "compromisers" is: "That is old fashioned; they believed that in the dark ages." This is precisely the religious situation. Divine Truth is more immutable than mathematical truth. There is only *one* Church just as there is only one multiplication table. Hence the problem of Church unity is not human agreement but divine agreement. The sects may change because they are man-made. The Church cannot, because it is God-made.

This brings us now to a more direct consideration of Western Civilization in relation to authority. Let it be stated at once that the present world attitude toward authority is quite different now from what it was at the time of the World War.[2]

_____

[2] "It was the Great War that brought to light many of the motives of national politics, that heretofore had been hidden behind clever ambitions. After this world-breakdown, old ideals were abandoned. The free-

The nineteenth century and the beginning of the twentieth century were distinctly anti-authoritarian. Like the Prodigal the world of those days threw off all authority, first the authority of the Church, then the authority of the Bible, and finally the authority of religion and morals in the political, economic, and social order. This break with authority created a false sense of liberty such as the Prodigal felt in the first wild moments of dissipation. Liberty was bound to be distorted once it was torn away from truth and responsibility. To be free became synonymous with doing whatever you pleased, whether it was good or evil, or believing whatever you pleased, whether it was true or false. The result was that freedom degenerated into a form of "selfishness," expressed itself in such slogans as "be yourself," frowned upon all forms of restraint and sacrifice as injurious to the individual *libido*, and ended in what might be called the exaltation and glorification of the ego.

The tremendous upheavals of the past few decades have made the world swing to the opposite extreme. From the one extreme of having no authority, it has now swung to the other extreme of having too much of it. The Prodigal soon discovered that his new-found freedom was only submission to another authority

---

dom of democracy was blamed for much that had miscarried; a reaction set in, and intensive ruling was inaugurated. Russia's system has all the strength of a monomania." — M. C. D'Arcy, S.J., *The Life of the Church*, pp. 323, 324.

than that of his father; namely, the slavery of his own passions. A man is always the slave of that which overcomes him. In like manner, the modern world has found that having rejected the authority of God it is now subject to the authority of Caesar. Such has always been the fact of history, and each new age must learn the sad lesson anew.[3]

What are the forces which produced this reaction toward authority? One is that men having dropped out of the harmony of life, and having lost the religious sanctions of authority, sought some obligatory organization as the sole means of avoiding final chaos and degeneration. Like camels who run together when frightened, so men of "rugged individualism," when frightened by the collapse of every ideal they believed to be true, sought refuge in the human collective, the mass or the State. *It was a way of trying to get collective control over that which should have been con-*

---

[3] "The rejection of Divine authority inevitably results in social decay; as this process goes on, society breaks up more and more, state authority intervenes, and in attempting to offset the evil, grows more and more tyrannical. Then the collapse, as history shows. "There is a deep lesson to be learned well by all today who are turning for social salvation to to 'totalitarian' state. *And* the lesson is that the state which becomes a mere end in itself, and subordinates all interests to itself, cannot but end by destroying its own foundations, like the snail that eats its own tail. Unless the new authoritarian state which we sorely need today (as Rome needed Caesar and Augustus) is a real expression of renewed social health, and unless it undertakes a truly radical social mission supported by a determined popular will, it will end as the Roman imperial state ended." — R. J. S. Hoffman, *The Will to Freedom*, pp. 109, 116 (New York: Sheed and Ward).

trolled by a social religion informing the individual conscience. The individual conscience in the Christian order should have frowned upon and rejected all social injustices. But with the conscience divorced from Christianity, and fear of God's judgment and all love of Eternal Life, each man in the language of St. Paul: "sought his own and not Christ's." The abuses reached such enormous proportions that political authority had to step in and re-establish itself over economic forces which had long escaped from it and were now mocking it. That is why the reaction against individualism tended to dictatorship.[4] In some nations it did not stop with the State attempting to enforce the legally just as a substitute for the morally righteous: it reached a point where the State assumed complete control over the temporal and spiritual life of man. A social conscience took the place of a personal conscience. Dictatorship overflowed into the spiritual order; organization became an obsession; social planning became a mania. A unity of ideas and belief was imposed upon the submerged personalities by the State, which felt the need of creating an economic unity to replace the spiritual unity whose basis is Christ.

The general effect of the reaction was the substitution of the authority of Caesar for the authority of God. We are *witnessing, therefore, the queer spectacle of a world that began four hundred years ago by*

------

[4] Reginald Tribe, *The Christian Social Tradition*, pp. 283, 284.

hating authority, now falling down before an author-
ity more absolute than history has seen since the ad-
vent of Christianity. The authority of the Father's
house was rejected because it was said to stand in the
way of liberty, and now the prodigal world finds itself
the slave of those forces it once thought would make
it free. It would not have God with His law of love,
now it must have Caesar with his iron law; it would
not be subject to the Father, now it must be subject
to the citizen of the foreign country.

The Prodigal discovered that there is no escaping
authority; and the modern world is now finding it
out again. Hence the problem is not whether we will
or will not accept authority; the problem is *which*
authority will we accept, the authority of Christ, or
the authority of the anti-Christ. Our age is now an-
swering that question.

There is nothing more misunderstood by the modern mind than the authority of the Church. Just as
soon as one mentions the authority of the Vicar of
Christ there are visions of slavery, intellectual servi-
tude, mental chains, tyrannical obedience, and blind
service on the part of those who, it is said, are forbidden to think for themselves. That is positively un-
true. Why has the world been so reluctant to accept
the authority of the Father's house? Why has it so
often identified the Catholic Church with intellectual
slavery? The answer is, because the world has forgotten the meaning of liberty. Freedom for the mod-

ern world means absence of all restraint; a perpetual vacation from authority, a holiday from law, and a right to believe whatever one pleases. Very simply, freedom for the modern mind is identified with indifference to truth. Hence, one religion is just as good as another, and contradictory principles are equally true depending on your point of view.

Freedom, however, is not absence from all law or restraint, but only liberty from those external forces which are hostile to the best and highest interests of my nature. Freedom does not mean to do whatever pleases, e.g., to dissipate, to rob, to steal, to blaspheme; it means to choose among various goods those which best conduce to your perfection. The Church refuses to identify freedom with either absence of restraint, or indifference to truth. On the contrary she insists that freedom has something to do with Truth. Such is precisely the message of our Lord: "The Truth will make you free."[5]

----

[5] "Liberty will be saved by its union with truth — it cannot be saved by indifference to Truth. Know the Truth and the Truth shall make you free. The age of skeptical liberty is closing, a new age is beginning. Freedom understood as something positive and joined with creativeness, becomes creative energy. Freedom means not only freedom of choice, but choice itself. Freedom cannot be simply a formal self-defense; it must lead to creative activity. The transition is inevitable from formal liberty, by which each protects and defends himself, to true freedom by means of which human society is creatively transfigured. But the transition to true and creative liberty means, first of all, not the rights of the citizen, but of man as a concrete and integral being, a being rooted in the spiritual order." — N. Berdyaev, *The Fate of Man in the Modern World*, pp. 38, 39 (Milwaukee: Morehouse Pub. Co.).

But how can Truth make us free? Truth makes us free because obedience to its dictates enables us to attain the highest perfection of our being. For example, the truth about a triangle is that it has three sides. Hence, I am free to draw a triangle only on condition that I obey the intrinsic law of its nature, and give it three sides, and not in a stroke of broadmindedness either four or forty sides. The truth about health is that the body must be nourished by food. The law of nature is absolute: I must eat to live. I cannot be so tolerant about that law as to eat only once a year. But suppose I obey that law of eating: suppose I subject myself to its restraining truth. What follows? I discover that I am free to live. Only those who accept the law of gravitation are free to fly; and only those who accept the truth of the meaning of words, are free to speak.

Now, we have not only a body but also a soul. What food is for the body, what color is to the eyes, what sound is to the ear, that truth is for the soul; namely, its perfection. I, therefore, become most free when I obey those truths which make for the highest development of my whole being, by submitting myself to all the laws and discipline by which life attains to fruition. Just as I am not free to live if I violently disobey the laws or the truth about health, so, too, I am not free to attain to the fullness of my whole being, except by correspondence to the truths of the physical, mental, and spiritual order in which I live, move, and have my being. Freedom is to be in possession of oneself.

This is the fact the Prodigal Son came to realize by sad experience; namely, it is vain to try to escape from all law. By throwing it aside he found that he became bound by other laws; namely, the passions and vicious habits to which he had subjected himself. So, too, with Western Civilization. It has been experimenting with liberty these past four hundred years, and now learns at last, that there is no such thing as freedom in the sense of absence of all restraint; it has found that freedom does not mean the right to violate the laws of God and man. The world identified freedom with indifference to truth, and now is lost in a maze of errors; it measured freedom in terms of absence of authority, and now finds that it was never before so subject to authority of a cruel and tyrannical kind; it wanted a society that was absolutely free, in which everyone could carry a gun if he wanted to, and found that such freedom made watchfulness a burden; it wanted an order in which every man was free, and found out too late that in such an order only the strong are free; it wanted a religion in which each man could think out his own beliefs, and found it just as absurd as thinking out his own astronomy.

There is now an increasing recognition of the fact that the Church may be the only place where there is real freedom.[6] It may once more be convinced, after the manner of the Prodigal, that the authority of the Father which he rejected as the barrier to freedom was the only authority which could ever make him free. And such is really the case. The Church is our Lord diffused through space and time; it is Christ living in His Mystical Body; it is the social prolongation of the second Person of the Blessed Trinity; it is the Body which is united to Him as branches to a vine, and through which He teaches now just as He taught through the instrumentality of His physical Body. The Church being Christ has no other philosophy of freedom than Christ Himself: "The Truth will make you free." These truths are few: e.g., the divinity of Christ, the necessity of a spiritual rebirth into His brotherhood, and others found in the Creed.[7] But these truths are absolute, eternal, irrevocable. They are made by God and hence cannot be unmade

---

[6] Those who look on certainly expect that "when the Catholic Christian handles a vital issue theoretically or practically, the situation should be immediately altered. . . . Every object brought into the Catholic sphere of influence and subjected to the Catholic spirit should recover its freedom and once more fully realize its nature. . . . I do not think that I am exaggerating the case. What else are those numerous men and women seeking in the Church, who are looking towards her today? No doubt some may be influenced by a romantic precosity; others, by the desire to find something solid in whatever quarter, without any genuine conviction that here, and here alone, truth is to be found; and fashion also plays its part, as in the influence in Buddhism on primitive cultures. This cannot be denied. But there is more than this. We can detect that expectation that in Catholicism the Essential — the Eternal, the Absolute — finds its due recognition." — Romano Guardini, *The Church and the Catholic*, pp. 67, 68 (New York: Sheed and Ward).

[7] Cf. L. Freund, *The Threat to European Culture*, pp. 126, 127.

by man; they are eternal, and hence cannot be changed
to suit the times; they are absolute and hence cannot
be modernized to suit the way men now live, for right
is right if nobody is right, and wrong is wrong if every-
body is wrong.

But outside of these essential truths which make a
man free to attain the fullness of his perfection as a
child of God and heir of the kingdom of heaven, a
Catholic is free to believe anything. As long as the
pendulum is fixed at one point, it can swing freely in
any direction. But it must be fixed at one point; so
long as a man accepts the truth, that two and two
make four, he is free to measure either his height or
the distance of the stars, but he must accept that truth
as fixed. In like manner, once the Catholic accepts the
eternal truths of Christ, he is free to accept all the
nonessential beliefs he pleases. He can be a monarchist
or a republican; he can live solitary and alone on a
pillar like Simon, or he can busy himself on the streets
of Paris like a Vincent de Paul; he can accept Einstein
or reject him; he can believe in the gold standard or
the silver standard; he can play cards and dance, or
he can abstain from them; he can drink moderately
or he can be prohibitionist. He is like a man living
on a great island in the sea on which he may roam and
exercise his freedom in a thousand and one games,
but only on condition that he obey the only law that is
posted there: Do not jump over the walls. But if he
ever thought freedom was denial of that one truth
and insisted on jumping over the walls, he would find

he was no longer free to play or sing or dance. Only the truth can make him free. And there is the difference between the Church and the world; in the Church one agrees on fundamentals, and differs about nonessentials; in the world one agrees on nonessentials and differs on fundamentals. In the Church one accepts truth and differs about moods; in the world one obeys moods and differs about truth. In the Church triangles have three sides, though they may be drawn in red or blue or green; in the world red is the rule of fashion, but it is indifferent whether you believe a triangle has three sides or not. This is no exaggeration: in the Church one believes that Christ is the Son of God, but whether one believes in futurism does not matter. In the world if one does not believe that everything is relative, even truth, he is considered behind the times, though it makes no difference what one believes about Him who came to die that the world might believe in His Truth. Catholics prefer the unchangeable truth that man has an unchangeable head; but we do not care a snap of our fingers what kind of hat he wears; he can change that to suit the fashions; but for the life of us, we cannot understand the world that wants to change its God because it discovers a new astronomy.

The Church during her exile has been attacked as the bitter enemy of liberty and freedom. Present-day facts reveal that she alone is the bulwark and guarantee of liberty, the only great institution standing which asserts that man is free. Every word she utters now is a protest against the new slavery. The new slavery is different from the old. The old slavery was *physical;* a man under that regime was not permitted to gather the fruits of the labor of his hands, or the rewards of the sweat of his brow; his work, his talents, his body, his wife, and his children belonged to the man who owned him. The new slavery is not physical, but *spiritual* and *moral;* it affects sometimes the body, as it does in Russia, but principally it affects the soul, the conscience, the will, and the personality of man; it takes its roots into the more *human* and *divine* part of him; asserts the primacy of the economic order over the human, and subjects him to the race, the class, the proletariat, the State which owns him, and whose dominant passion is the passion for power.

Against this new slavery, whose venom strikes deeper roots than the old, the Church has risen in protest. Why has she condemned birth control, sterilization? why has she anathematized Communism? and Nazism? why has she condemned employers who would deny workmen the right to organize? why has she frowned upon workmen who would abolish all private property? Simply because each of these things are violations of the rights of man; because a human personality has certain inalienable rights which no one can take away from him; in a word, because a man is to be measured and judged, not by what he produces for the State, but by what he is destined to be by God.

This is a new role for the Church. Yes, she has had

to defend liberties before, but they were liberties of the supernatural order. Up until the close of the nineteenth century she had to assert the freedom of a man to accept grace, against Calvinistic determinism. But now she is called upon, not to defend liberty in the order of grace, but liberty in the order of nature; now she is summoned forth to battle not for the freedom of *a man to be a saint,* but for the freedom of a man *to be a man.* This is a sad state of affairs, when Christ in His Mystical Body has to remind the world of those truths which even the pagans believed; namely, the right of a man to be free, to be captain of his own soul.

If the world continues to get so far away from fundamentals, a day may yet come when the Church will go out to battle in defense of the truth that two and two make four. Her excommunications of the future will not be against those who deny that there are three persons in God, but against those who deny that every citizen in a State is a person. She has been the defender of the revealed liberties of the world; now, she is to be the defender of the last liberty of all, the freedom of man.

Rob man of the freedom of serving and loving God and you have robbed him of his manhood. Men with minds that can fly, cannot be kept in cages; men with Divine homesickness cannot find homes under roofs; men destined to be filled with Life and Truth and Love, cannot be satisfied with their bellies filled. Rob them of their God, which is the root of all the liberties of man, and they will build a false god as they are doing now. When Moses was absent for forty days on the mountaintop communing with the Living God, the children of Israel made for themselves a golden calf. And today when the people of Russia and Germany are deprived of God, they make for themselves the iron calf of the State and the race; if they are not permitted to walk in processions to the Mother of God, they will dance about tractors; if they are forbidden to adore God in a tabernacle, they will bow down before an embalmed corpse and a paraffined cheek in the Kremlin of the Red Square. That is why the Communism of Russia is the opium of the people,[8] it does not deny God who was the root of all their

---

[8] "Both Marx's famous dictum, 'Religion is opium for the people' and that of Lenin, 'Religion is alcohol' bespeak the hostility toward religion in Russia. As the Marxians understand it, the masses cannot realize the actual social condition, because religion screens it from their eyes; nor do they see social reality as it is, because they are exploited by Capitalism. Religion has the deadening effect of a drug because it holds out hope or makes endurable the suffering of life. For Marxism there is no hope beyond society itself. To look for any reality beyond this life is impossible. Reality is making an all-sufficient society and for the accomplishment of this, Marxism must struggle against religion. Religion for the Marxian means nothing more than a distortion of reality, or a fetish in Marx's own words. It is tied up with the supremacy of Capitalism, trade, and money. But as the true reality, the socialist society comes to its full self, religion and her capitalistic company must pass. In other words, religion is not an essential part of men, but only a symptom of diseased social conditions, which will vanish with the restoration of social health." — Waldemar Gurian, *Bolshevism: Theory and Practice,* pp. 222–224 (New York: Sheed and Ward).

liberties; it falsified His image, and makes them slaves. But this will not satisfy them long. Communism may build Babels, a thousand factories, schools, and hospitals, but their Babels will crumble without the Cornerstone; the products of their factories will be without excellence, the dying in their hospitals will not be healed, the scholars in their schools will not learn Wisdom, because they have forgotten that a cow is satisfied because its stomach is full, but not a man.

❁❁❁

Chapter VII

THE SENSE OF SIN

THE final condition of the return to the Father's house is a recognition of the sense of sin. After having entered into himself, and after having admitted a need for spiritual pabulum and the freedom which authority alone can purchase, the Prodigal said: "I will go to my Father": "I have sinned against heaven and before thee; I am not worthy to be called thy son; make me as one of thy hired servants." Herein is combined the double element of true redemption, and admission of sin: "I have sinned," and the need of penance, "make me as one of thy hired servants."

Our Blessed Lord never once hints in the parable that, when the young man returned, with a face furrowed with the hard lines of sin, he offered an excuse for his sinfulness. There is no record, there is not even a hint, that he attempted to excuse himself or to extenuate his prodigality. He offered no theory about sin; he did not blame his wicked companions; he did not tell his father that he had inherited a queer complex; he did not say that moral decline is only a myth and that sin is just an illusion; he offered no case to prove that moral lapses are pardonable, nor that the great broad world of experience had told him that man was just to sow his wild oats and then forget, live for the future, and have no responsibility toward the past. There were none of these things in the mouth of the Prodigal, and much less was there any such thought in his heart, but only a deep recognition of the horror of sin, and a need of pardon and redemption. "I have sinned against heaven and before thee."

The sense of sin is one of the great and crying needs of the prodigal Western Civilization. It has not yet reached the stage of the Prodigal Son who offered no excuses or extenuation of sin, but it must reach that stage if it is ever to return. The Prodigal did not blame his father, nor his companions, nor his own physical make-up, but Western Civilization is blaming precisely these three things; it places the responsibility for guilt on everything except where it should be placed; namely, in self-will. The Prodigal did not blame his father; but Western Civilization, if it finds sin, does blame the father in the sense that it fixes practically the whole guilt for sin on heredity, which can explain, of course, certain weak tendencies, but cannot wholly explain the guilt. The Prodigal did not blame his evil companions, but Western Civilization does, in the sense that it blames society and environment, which, of course, does play a part in making sin easier but never absolutely constrains the will to give way to it. The Prodigal did not blame his physical self, but Modern Civilization does so, in the sense that it invents very high-sounding names such as the Oedipus complex, introvert, and extrovert, to explain away sin, as if calling a sore throat a streptococcus infection would explain away the sore throat.

It may be interesting to inquire at this point why the modern world has lost its sense of sin. It should be immediately evident that it is the obvious consequence of the loss of the value of man. Under traditional Christianity, a man was a theological creature, an adopted son of God and a member of the Mystical Body of Christ; in the eighteenth and nineteenth centuries man became a philosophical thing bound to God by some vague ties of creaturehood. But man today is only a biological phenomenon with no other destiny than that of the worm he crushes under his heel. Once one loses hold on the primary dogma that man has a moral end, and that his actions, thoughts, and words in this life are all registered in the Book of Life, and therefore will one day determine his eternal destiny, sin becomes meaningless. The modern mind has forgotten the dogma of man, and hence cannot avoid forgetting the morals of man, for one is the corollary of the other. Deny that God is interested in the behavior of men and you immediately create a society in which man is uninterested in the behavior of his fellow man.

The great mistake of the nineteenth century was to believe that the intellectual basis of Christian doctrine about God and man, and their mutual relations, could be abolished without in any way impairing morals. Dogmas were considered impossible, but ethics were indispensable; doctrine was ridiculous but morals sublime; the Cross was folly, but the Sermon on the Mount was a masterpiece. Practically all advanced Victorian minds proceeded on the assumption that you could obliterate the religious beliefs of a nation without affecting its moral standards. It may take a generation or two to prove the fallacy of the statement: "It makes no difference what you believe; what matters is how you live"; but the world sooner or later discovers that it does make a difference, for we act on our beliefs, and if we think wrongly, we act wrongly.[1] If we do not suit our lives to dogmas, we will end by suiting dogmas to our lives.

Minds no longer object to the Church, because of the way they *think*, but because of the way they *live*. They no longer have difficulty with the Creed, but

---

[1] "This is the task of Catholicism: to purify our thinking, and so straighten out human conduct. She is endeavoring to bring back the *philosophia perennis*, also an *economia perennis*, which will bear the stamp of ethics and serve human not material ends, a Christian-like politics with due regard for personal rights and communal duties, and a sociology which will be in harmony with man's true nature. The Church as the deposit of truth takes the initiative. In many encyclicals she has condemned the false metaphysics of the moderns; for unless the domain of thought be purified, action will be bad." — Jacques Maritain, *Freedom in the Modern World*, p. 100 (New York: Scribners).

with her Commandments; they remain outside her saving waters, not because they cannot accept the doctrine of Three Persons in One God, but because they cannot accept the moral of two persons in one flesh; not because Infallibility is too complex, but because the veto on Birth Control is too hard; not because the Eucharist is too sublime, but because Penance is too exacting. Briefly, the heresy of our day is not the heresy of thought; it is the heresy of action.

We are living in a time when the old forms of sensationalism of a generation ago are now regarded as banal; words such as "obedience," "honor," and "purity," which once stood for the desirable and the sacred, now stand either for weakness, or restraint of liberty. Everything that is good, everything that is just, everything that is noble in our civilization is a reflection of abiding Christian principles. But they are fading away; the borderland between light and darkness is growing dimmer, and we are about to pass over into the hinterland of darkness and ruin. As a matter of fact, there has been a greater de-Christianization of society in the past hundred years than in any other given period of Christian history. As an evidence of how much God and morality have passed out of contemporary civilization, contrast two works, one written in the beginning of the fifth century, the other in the beginning of the nineteenth; namely, *The City of God* of St. Augustine and the *Philosophy of History* of Frederick Schlegel. The first is manifestly more

spiritual, but there is common to both, an admission
that the purposes of God work themselves out in history, and that civilization is unintelligible without the
Lord of the Universe.

Now contrast two works written in the past hundred years, almost to the exact year. *The Philosophy
of History* of Schlegel which was just mentioned, and
the *Outline of History* by H. G. Wells. The Providence of God mattered in the first, but it is not even
mentioned in the second. Today there is a general
atrophy of a vital conviction that there is a righteous
purpose sovereign in history. Men today model their
lives solely in relation to economic interest rather than
the common good and the glory of God.

There is probably no greater proof of the decline
of the idea of sin than the widespread popularity of
Marxism. There is some similarity between Rousseau
and Marx in the sense that both thought man naturally good in the theological sense of the term.
Rousseau said man was born good but society ruined
him; Marx said man was born good, but capitalism
ruined him. Society and capitalism both take the
place of original sin. Rousseau "redeemed" man by
the "Social Contract," and Marx by the "Classless
Class" or the proletarian revolution.

The proletariat became the new elect for Marx
very much as the bourgeoisie became the elect for
Calvin, with this difference. Election for Calvin was
by the predestination of God; election for Marx is

by materialism. All the modern solutions since the
days of Rousseau have gone wrong by forgetting man
is a fallen creature. Marx thinks that by eliminating
Capitalism, he establishes original justice. It is sheer
illusion to think that the new order will eliminate
social injustices and restore the peace of the original
Paradise. Man has sinned before and he will sin again,
and Communism is no redemption for sin; it is only
forced tranquillity.

What adds to the seriousness of this view is that the
world's fallen state is accompanied, not by an increased, but by a decreased sense of sin. The world
sins more, but is less mindful of its seriousness. Paganism sinned, too, but the sin of modern paganism has
the added seriousness of having betrayed an ideal
which the older pagans had not; namely, the ideal of
Christ.

By this I do mean to say that when the world accepted the faith and morals of the Church, that the
world was free of sinners. As a matter of fact there
were men just as wicked in the thirteenth century as
there are in the twentieth; there were souls just as
immoral in the second century as there are today. But
there is this great difference between the sinners of a
Christianized civilization and the sinners of our day:
the sinners of the Christian civilization *knew they
were sinners;* the sinners of modern civilization think
they are saints; the sinners of the Christian civilization broke the law, but admitted the *law was right;*

the sinners of modern civilization break the law, and say that the law is wrong. The sinners of Christian ages knew they were wrong, and wished they were right. The sinners of our day, on the contrary, do wrong, but do not want to be right. As we have already seen, there is hope for any civilization which breaks a law but never calls in question the truth of the law; but there is no hope for a civilization that breaks a law and then denies it.

Man is powerless to resist evil if he does not recognize it as such, and deceives himself when he becomes indifferent to evil; his whole personality immediately begins to dissolve, for the power of conscience is inseparably bound up with the denunciation of evil. And this is precisely what our world is doing today; the very beliefs on which the best culture of the world was built are now called in question. Even the distinction between good and evil is lost, and now only a sense of civic loyalty remains. The Prophet Isaias sounded such a decadence in his day: "Woe to you that call evil good, and good evil; that put darkness for light, and light for darkness; that put bitter for sweet and sweet for bitter."

If we called sin by its right name it would lose all of its seductiveness. Hell can be made attractive, only by surfacing it with the gold of Paradise. It is unfortunate indeed that those who think unspeakable filth, have the gift of writing good English. Their readers feel they are justified in reading the book because the

style is good. We might just as well say that it is per-
missible to take poison provided it is sugar coated.

Now this loss of the sense of sin is serious. Civilization begins to go to pieces when it loses its respect and
love for saints and begins to interest itself in the lives
of criminals. Lecky, in his *History of European Morals*,
writes in a very eloquent passage that, "While the
Greek and Roman world was perplexed by the mystery of being, and shadowed by the suffering of life,
and while it was moved by the examples of great
heroism, there was no sense of sin possessing men's
hearts. Remorse was an unknown passion, and penitent shame was impossible. The burden of guilt did
not rest on even a criminal's heart. Men looked on
deeds of infamy and were not shocked. The sin of
the world and its moral corruption infected the air.
Men were naked and not ashamed, not because they
were innocent, but because no sense of guilt assailed
them."

Just how far the world has departed from the standard of the Cross one need hardly ask. How seldom does
one find anyone outside the Father's house doing penance for his sins, i.e., applying the Cross of Christ to his
soul? How often does a writer of immoral books,
when he comes to a consciousness of the souls he has
polluted, end his days in prayer and reparation? How
often does a man who has gained great wealth unjustly, ever think of setting his soul right with God?

Rarely indeed is it recorded in the twentieth century of a sinner seeking to enter the kingdom of God by doing penance. It is rare, because the modern ideal has changed. The absolute ideal no longer is goodness, but success. The poor man may be good, but to the modern mind, he has failed if he is unsuccessful. Such an ideal renders penance and the desire of redemption impossible. The modern man is grateful so long as he does not die poor, for to him "what doth it profit a man if he save his soul and lose the whole world?" His deathbed is one of unctuous self-esteem and self-complacency, but never a cry for the mercy and love of God.

It is no wonder that Communism has decided to make a clean sweep of what it calls "bourgeois morality," which is really only a flimsy sentimentalism expressed by catchwords such as "leave the world better than you find it." Communism must be given the credit of seeing the fallacy of morals divorced from a dogmatic basis, and that basis it has tried to supply. For Communism an act is good if it subserves the economic prosperity of the State. The final end in such a system of morality is the political collective. The test of any act is the good of the State.

But even this moral code is just as unsatisfactory as the "higher-living" ideal of the "bourgeois moralists." The question they have to answer is this: What is the final good of the proletariat State? Why slave and work? Why permit personality and freedom for cultural and religious pursuits to be strangled for the good of the

State? What will eventually happen to the State? According to the second law of thermodynamics, the State is one day destined to perish, and with it all the little human cogwheels that made its big flywheel spin. But if the State is destined to die, then the final end of a good and bad action are the same; namely, death and dissolution.[2] If the waves of the seas are to wash away the sandcastles built on the shore, what difference does it make if I build them six feet tall or six inches tall? If all our actions are to be cursed with a gigantic futility, why do good rather than evil; why work for the economic good of the State which will perish, rather than my own economic good which will also fade into dust?

Communism cracks at that one point: What is the use of economically dominating the earth if we cannot take it with us? The death of man renders all our Titanism and worldly conquest mean and negligible. A funeral for that reason is the expression of the futility of the Communistic State for in the presence of every corpse, men will ask themselves: "What doth it profit to gain the whole world?" Joseph Roth in his book *Anti-Christ* pictures Death speaking to the body of Lenin, whose corpse the Communists conquered even though they could not conquer death. That corpse, the author says is "like an ostentatious, but, of course, at the same time childish threat to Death, who is shown that his victim can none the less be pre-

---

[2] Cf. Nicholas Berdyaev, *The End of Our Time*, pp. 113-115, 183.

served — like jewelry which is no longer worn." Death speaks and says: "Your threat is childish and your pride is folly. It is my task to take from this earth not his countenance but that which was his life and which you love; namely, his breath. He is extinguished, like a lamp. I have taken wick and oil, and you may keep the vessel, with which I am not concerned. It was his flame which you loved, and his light! Why are you now flaunting the insignificant vessel in which they were contained? Many great lights have I already extinguished, and monuments were erected to them. That is wiser than what you are doing! For a monument does not deny, but confirms the law according to which I act. And because it confirms me, it also conquers me. A monument, however cheap, is the sign that the living remember the dead, and it is an impotent but reverent form of resurrection. You, however, do not cause the dead man to be resurrected. You give permanence to his corpse and refuse to let it molder. Why should a corpse not fall into dust and ashes? Did man come from paraffin and wax, to become once more paraffin and wax? If you have as much respect for the dead man as you say you have, do you not comprehend that he should not be exhibited as a barber exhibits his wigs or wax busts Why do you flaunt your achievement in my face — in the face of Death? You have withheld nothing from me, but you have detracted from your own dignity — your own, and that of your dead."

The most terrible consequence of the loss of the sense of sin, as was hinted above, is that it destroys the yearning for redemption, for a man who does not know cancer is devouring him, feels no need of a physician. During the last century the theory of evolution applied to sociology, resulted in the false idea of "progress"[3] which led men to believe that cosmic laws guaranteed his necessary and inevitable perfection. In those days of progress, man had faith in tomorrow, faith in big business, faith in science, faith in utilitarian education, faith in common sense, faith in faith. When "progress" cracked, all the baseless duties of unreasonable faith collapsed, and we found ourselves not evolving but dissolving. The notion of the "inevitable" then substituted itself for "progress." Having lost the purposiveness of human life in relation to the beatific vision, faith gave way to despair. Now men feel they are caught in the web of circumstances and that decay must eventually work itself out before things become better.

This is where the doctrine of Redemption asserts itself, as the antithesis of despair. It provides in the final place, an explanation for the failure of the law of progress, by giving an explanation of the otherwise unaccountable fact, that what the good men will to do, that, they do not; and the evil which they will not,

---

[3] Cf. Maritain, Wust, Dawson, *Essays in Order,* General Introduction, XI–XII; cf. also Maritain, *The Things That Are Not Caesar's,* App. V, "On Liberalism."

that, they do.[4] Secondly, it provides an escape from the "inevitable," by assuring us that the most important thing about sin is not its sinfulness, but the fact that it can be atoned. Man need not slide down to ruin; he need not be the plaything of circumstances; he can be remade, reshaped, and redeemed for nobler ends, for within history there is a Redeemer.

Redemption is not an exclusively individual affair between God and the soul; it does not merely entail

------

[4] Here the Catholic point of view stresses the order of sin, and the order of grace. Too often they both are overlooked. A solution to our social evils must recognize both. Man in his fallen or natural state is prone to evil, but raised to the supernatural state by grace, he can hope for strength to overcome himself. In Adam we are subject to our nature; in Christ we are masters of our senses. Ovid: "I see the better things of life; I follow the wicked." As noted, man is a member of the society of Adam and the society of Christ. The human race as a society has its natural head in Adam and its spiritual head in Christ. The members joined to the head constitute the body (*De Malo*, q. 4, art. 1). Therefore, there are two bodies, one after the flesh, the other after the spirit. When the head of the former body, Adam, sinned, original sin passed on to us, not as a personal sin, but as a sin of nature; when Christ paid the price of redemption, His graces came to us. If no Adam, there would be no human race; if no Christ, there would be no regenerated humanity. With this understanding, our conclusion is that the members of Christ's body can speak of victory, when they build the City of God and not the City of Man. However, the primal curse of humanity cannot be ignored. Pope Leo XIII (*Rerum Novarum*) points out that "to suffer and endure is the lot of humanity. . . . If there are any who pretend differently . . . they delude the people. . . . Nothing is more useful than to look upon the world as it really is and at the same time to look elsewhere for a solace for its troubles."

See Sheen, F. J., *The Mystical Body*, note 1, 35; also notes 2 and 3, 36.

Leo XIII in his Encyclical *Exeunte Jam Anno*, gives due treatment to original sin and its consequences as affecting the ordering of Christian life.

faithfulness to the ethical teachings of our Lord, nor constitute only a challenge to overcome our individual difficulties. Redemption is something social as well as personal, for man is a member of society. To proclaim its social character, He who came unto His own and was rejected, set up His Cross, not in the individual heart, but in the world; it was placarded before the eyes of men, in the open air, under the noonday sun, at the very crossroads of civilization, to remind us all that our destiny is the kingdom of God.

That Cross was so social it began a new world; it gave men new standards of living, a new way of measuring and judging the sorrows and trials of this life; it offered a different balance in which to weigh the earth against their souls. It gave men a fresh start, even though it was a late start, another hope, a safer orientation, a brighter vision, and it did all this, because it was so very revolutionary. It upset worldly standards as the Lord one day upset the tables of the money-changers in the Temple; it made the first last, and the last first; exalted the humble, and humbled the exalted; made enemies loved and blessed persecutors; forgave the sinners and put a premium on losing a life in order to save it. Looking down the corridors of time, it made all subsequent revolutions but trivial upstarts, for they failed to affect the soul of society; even the Communistic revolution was incomplete for it still leaves hate and does not say, "forgive"; it still leaves earthliness and does not say: "This day thou shalt be with Me in Paradise"; it still leaves despair, and does not say: "Father, into Thy hands I commend My spirit."

Now this redemptive love of the cross did not stop with the Good Friday of nineteen hundred years ago; as long as sin remains the Cross still stands. Until the last sheaf is garnered into the everlasting barns, the Reaper of souls remains in the field. The souls, such as that of the penitent thief, won on that first day of the cross, and the souls won ever since by grace issuing from that cross constitute the kingdom of God, or the Mystical Body of Christ. The members of this society did not create the kingdom of God; the kingdom of God in Christ the First Born pre-existed them. The condition of incorporation with the Mystical Body of Christ is the acceptance not merely of the ethical teachings of our Lord, but the acceptance of the Cross and all that it means: "If any man will come after Me, let him deny himself, and take up his cross and follow Me." "They that are Christ's have crucified their flesh with its vices and concupiscences." This corporation of the lovers of the cross under the inspiration of the Crucified, institutes the new society through which Christ redeems the world. It is the new humanity, the spiritual corporation, in which each individual draws his strength directly from Christ Himself through the Mass which is Calvary re-enacted and through the Sacraments which are Calvary distributed.

This Mystical Body of Christ which accepts the

revolutionary standard of the Cross, is the leaven in the mass of the world, revealing to each man the true end of life; it is to the new world what Judaism was to the Gentiles, what the soul is to the body, what light is to darkness — the channel of social regeneration. It does not make everyone in the world saintly, for man is still free; it does not make everyone a lover of the Cross, for many are still selfish; it does not relieve the world of suffering, for its kingdom of happiness is not in this world; it has not saved modern civilization, because modern civilization has not tried it, but only its substitute, and imitations. However, it does secure a recognition of a supernatural criterion and a normal pattern of life, which, if accepted, would enable the mass of men to fulfill their destiny on earth without being obliged to impossible heroism; it does provide an eternal end rather than a temporal end, as the basis of social action, and that means everything; it does make life reasonable by assuring man that he lives in a world of good and evil opportunity, where his choice must be a matter of significance for himself and his fellow men; it does influence the economic order by condemning the idiocy of burning wheat in a land of hunger, and of calling men "superfluous" in a universe where every man has an immortal soul; and suppressing man for the sake of the State when a man is a citizen of the kingdom of God, as well as the kingdom of Caesar.

The social character of the Redemption is based on the principle that "the same Christ is assuredly the source of the individual's salvation; neither is there a salvation in any other, for there is no other name under heaven, given to men whereby we may be saved." He is the author of prosperity and of genuine happiness for every citizen and for the nation. The happiness of the State comes from exactly the same source as the happiness of the individual, the State being nothing else than a number of individuals living in harmony. The faithful, moreover, by diligently meditating on these matters will gain much strength and courage, enabling them to fashion their own lives on the true Christian ideal. For if to Christ our Lord is given all power in heaven and on earth; and if this power that Christ wields is exercised over human nature in its entirety, it is abundantly clear that not one of our faculties is exempt from His all-embracing sovereign sway. "He must reign in the mind of man, which ought to assent with perfect submission and firm, unwavering belief to the revealed truths and doctrines of Christ. He must reign in man's will, which ought to obey the laws and precepts of God. He must reign in the heart of man, which ought to reject the cravings of nature and love God above all things and cleave to Him alone. He must reign in the body and in its members, which ought to serve as instruments towards the interior sanctification of our souls, or as the Apostle Paul says, of instruments of justice unto God."[5]

------

[5] Encyclical of Pius XI on the *Kingship of Christ.*

The redemptive society of the Mystical Body of Christ is not a movement of social reform; it is not a sentimental loyalty toward which men may turn after all human remedies have failed; rather it is the regeneration of society through the spiritual rebirth of the men and women who compose it. Social order is not organized from the outside but vivified from the inside[6] by giving human life a meaning and a spiritual significance. Political alliances, economic plans prom-

---

[6] "Péguy says: 'The social revolution will be a moral revolution or none at all.' He does not mean that *all* men must be converted before the social order can be re-established. Reforms are the work of a few, but intensive work. Each begins the work within his own soul, whence it goes out to those around. We point out two opposite dangers in this procedure, looking for holiness only in the desert, and forgetting the need of the desert for holiness. There is a tendency to house up virtue selfishly, and not bother about the rest of mankind; and again, when it is shared, to dissipate it by worldly standards. It is high time that Christian sanctity make itself felt. Does our age stand any chance of seeing a new temporal order based on Christianity? Quite assuredly, it will not be achieved like other events of the temporal order. The renewal will be moral or not at all.

"With this reflection arises a problem. Since the reform rests with a small number, will it be the work of the Church, or of Catholic Action, i.e., the lay apostolate? It is clear that the revolution of the temporal regime cannot be the concern of the Church, whose end is spiritual and whose interests are beyond political and social issues. For the same reason neither can Catholic Action, itself subject to the hierarchy of the Church, so busy itself. Now do not let it be thought that Catholic Action has no interest whatever in the temporal crises. Far from it. But when its spiritual order comes in touch with the temporal order, its presence is felt, and its spiritual values determine the social, political, and economic values. It is the soul-principle actuating the body-order of the temporal. Indirectly, but no less effectively, it leads to the direct end, that of Christian truth." — Jacques Maritain, *Freedom in the Modern World,* pp. 142–151.

ise quicker results but they are bound to fail so long as society pins its faith in material ends, and appeals only to utilitarian sanctions. The meaning and spiritual significance of society can be supplied only by the Cross. Human society may continue to offer men the *means* of existence, but the Church with its Cross alone can offer the *object* of existence which determines the morality of the means. Man has indeed missed the mark, but there is a mark; and that mark is to be attained not through a higher will, but through a new level of being and a new energy brought to man through the Person of Christ, and made available through His social existence in His Church.

It may take the modern world a long time before it is willing to cry out with the Prodigal: "I have sinned," but until that day arrives it can expect no healing ointment for its broken wings. There is no redemption except from sin; there is no hope for betterment until there has been an admission of failure. Our social structure, then, must one day admit the fallacy of "business is business"; it must judge its economic policies not by their feasibility but by their morality; and it must confess that economics and politics are but branches of moral theology and philosophy, i.e., they can be sinful if they violate the ultimate end of man. The moral necessity of man's attaining the full perfection of his personality circumscribes human action in the domestic, political, economic, and religious spheres. Every act is a moral act, even a religious act;

nothing is excluded whether it be the selling of a can
of milk, or the formation of a great corporation. Hence
economic policy can save a man's soul as well as damn
it. Morality is involved in the realities of industries,
finances, and government, and the assumption that
these things are governed by non-ethical forces, is false.
Business can crucify Christ just as well as pride, and
therefore it has just as much need of redemption.

The ignoring of the moral basis of the economic
order, and therefore the denial of sin, has been the
conspicuous attitude of the social order for many
decades, during which time society has ignored the
Christian pattern of life. In that time the elements
of collapse have gathered on all sides: the loss of
human purpose, the dissatisfaction of the masses, the
glorification of the economic end, the loosening of
the moral bonds and the gradual dehumanization of
men in the great collective. And what is to be done
about it? What would we do if we found a live salmon
on top of the Empire State Building? We would try
to restore it as quickly as possible to its environment.
And that is the only thing to be done with the world.
Put it back in its environment of religion and morality. And all the discussion about politics and economics divorced from the moral order is just as stupid as
to legislate for salmon on skyscrapers. It is a change
of heart, of mind, of soul, and not exclusively a new
economics which is needed; and this new heart can
be found only at the foot of the Cross where things

are measured according to their true worth. Once men
see that Cross elevated before their eyes at the eleva-
tion of the host, they begin to realize that three score
and ten years of life is a time for testing — a moment
taken out of eternal life in which to say "yea" or "nay"
to Divine Love. We have been living for some time
on the margin of Christianity, but now the Cross is
beginning to fade from the eyes of men. The result
is we are face to face with disturbances from which
the earlier generations were saved. We must now
choose between having society radically rearranged by
the forces of sin which crucify, or spiritually regenerated by the Cross which redeems.

At the present moment, whether we admit it or not,
there is only one Power which stands between the
modern world and absolute chaos and decay, and that
is the Power of Christ in the Mass with His arms and
ours outstretched to the Heavenly Father making in-
tercession for the world. Suspended between heaven
and earth, He reconciles the two by something which
is not wholly of either, and yet of both. That Power
alone is left to declare unto the world that the life of
man is fraught with wonderful and holy purposes, and
that even though sin doth abound, saving grace and
redemption may yet more abound. There is no escaping the Cross, for the simple reason that there is no
goal gained without the effort, and no victory won
without the battle. To keep whispering to ourselves
sweet but false consolations, to look for the end when

we are only at the beginning, to go round the Cross instead of climbing on, these are but the materials out of which a cross is made — and a cross where one bar is at variance and contradiction with another, the most insoluble mystery of all.

But we must enter into that higher plane of making earth a steppingstone to heaven, where nobility stands the test, where love spells sacrifice, where the horizontal bar of death meets the vertical bar of life in the Person of Christ on the Cross reconciling both. This is the Crucifix wherein we confess not the mysterious ways of Job, but enter into them for our eternal joy and consolation. Once united with the Crucified as we are in the Mass, we begin to understand, that everywhere else, others promise us sin excused, sin discounted, sin denied, sin explained away, but only at the foot of the Cross do we ever experience the beautiful Divine contradiction of sin forgiven.

Chapter VIII

THE CHURCH AND THE STATE

THE Prodigal has now completed the four steps of conversion: (*a*) he entered into himself; (*b*) he acknowledged the need of supernatural life by his yearning for the Bread of the Father's House; (*c*) he saw that freedom was inseparable from truth and law; (*d*) finally, he admitted sin and the need of forgiveness.

Civilization must also take these four steps before it can recover its lost heritage; it must enter into itself and see that a man is not a tool of the economic order, but a creature made to the image and likeness of God; it must rebuild society on a basis of fellowship rather than equality, as suggested by the Eucharist; it must seek freedom in terms of truth rather than in terms of "self-expression"; finally, it must revise its standards in the light of the Cross which is at once the measure of the world's sin and the pledge of its redemption.

It now remains to inquire into the neighbor's attitude toward the Father's house. This entails a discussion of the Church and State. This chapter is concerned with the attitude of the new collectivist State to the

Church; the final chapter with the attitude of the Church to the collectivist State and the world.

The Father met the Prodigal on the road, when he was "yet a great way off." This implies that during the absence, the Father was hopeful, otherwise he would not have been on the road awaiting the return. The fatherly forebearance is like that taught in the parable of the barren fig tree. The owner of a garden noticed that one of his fig trees had borne no fruit for three years, and therefore ordered his gardener to cut it down, and clear it out of the way. "No," said the gardener, "let it alone this year also until I dig about it and dung it. And if happily it bear fruit; but if not, then after shalt thou cut it down." The Father was more glad at receiving the Prodigal home than he was in the elder son who always remained under the paternal roof. So the angels rejoice more at "one sinner doing penance than ninety-nine just who need not penance."

There may be somewhat the same *felix culpa* in prodigal Western Civilization. Western Civilization for several centuries has refused to have anything to do with the Church and its seven vivifying sacraments; it has contented itself with aspects of its truth, such as the Bible, preaching and hymn singing, public prayers, and the like. During this time the world has ignored the Church, and yet this exile of the Church from the social, economic, and political life of the world has had its advantages; it has, for one thing, been a punishment for the Church's worldliness at the time of the Reformation; secondly, it has enabled the Church to differentiate itself more and more from its spurious counterparts which resembled it sufficiently for a while to attract men who wished to be Christians. Now the Church is thrust into the foreground not only by the insignificance of her rivals, but also by the uniqueness of her claims. She is standing today before men as Christ stood before them; namely, as a thing to be either infinitely hated, or a thing to be infinitely loved, for such is the mark of Divinity.

The Church from the very beginning of her life on Pentecost has never ceased to be the object of attack and calumny. On that day men said the Apostles were drunk, and a short time afterward killed Stephen the deacon. Her mission is the mission of sheep among wolves and an apostolate in a world that hates. "I have taken you out of the world, therefore the world will hate you." But though the attack has been constant, the same weapons have not always been used. Taking a broad sweep of history, the first few centuries of the Church saw her attacked by the enemy of force which was persecution, the sword, the rack, and the wild beast. From the end of the persecutions on until modern times the attack was intellectual — she was not so much opposed by the sword as by the mind; the enemy was not from without but from within; it was not a Nero but a Nestorius, not a hammer, but a heresy, that would smite her down. In our days, the attack of force still lingers in some places, while the attack of heresy has almost completely died out.

Leaving the general for the more particular assaults of our days, we notice the same shifting of opposition. It is generally true to say that in the seventeenth century the Church was attacked as the enemy of the Bible; now she is attacked because she is so old fashioned as to believe in the Bible as the revealed word of God. In the eighteenth century the Church was attacked as the enemy of history, because she insisted on her extrahistorical or divine origin. Now she is attacked because she believes in history, respects tradition, and summons the dead to sit at her councils. In the late nineteenth century the Church was attacked as the enemy of Science and Reason. Now she is attacked because she believes in reason and refuses to subordinate it to nonintellectual approaches to God, such as the vague mysticism of the modern physicists.

The conclusion is that the Church presents herself as the enemy of the contemporary. The futurist condemns her for belonging to the present; the present condemns her for belonging to the past. She lives to see all the errors proved wrong, but never convinces any age that she is right. She suits no one time and no particular place. She refuses to be identified with the modernism of 1938 or the ideals of any one nation. Why does she suit no one time and no one place? Because she is outside all time, or eternal, and because she is outside all nationalities, or catholic. Like the soul in the body she is catholic, vivifying every member in her body without being localized in any particular member. "In every age," says Guardini, "she opposes the Here and Now for the Forever, and the Here and There for the Hereafter. Her seeming obscurantism is due to the way eternity reflects itself in time, and the way immensity breaks up into space."

In the past four hundred years the Church has had a decreasing number of common denominators with those outside her fold. There once was a time when a Catholic could argue with a Presbyterian on the basis of Sacred Scripture for both believed it to be the word of God. Today a Catholic cannot be sure that the Presbyterian will regard Scripture as any more inspired than Hamlet. Some time ago there was the common denominator of history, but today the modern man has no use for history; he is not interested in origins, but only in progress, quite forgetful that the origin of a thing is the measure to a great extent of the progress it will make. An acorn will make an oak, but not a coconut. Until recently the common denominator of all men was reason, but with Eddington, Jeans, Bergson, and others repudiating reason in favor of the mystical approach, the Catholic can no longer be sure he is arguing with one who believes in reason. When St. Thomas wrote his *Contra Gentiles,* he stated at the beginning, that he could not argue with the Moors on the grounds of Sacred Scripture, for it was not held in common by both. But he said both Christians and Moors believed in reason, therefore he would argue with them only on that ground. If St. Thomas wrote today, he could not be sure that his opponent believed in reason. He would probably find his opponent beginning with faith without having a reason for it, or starting with mysticism without being sure there was a God. This decrease in common denominators between the Church and the world is an evidence of the liquidation of Christian sects.

The world Catholics live in today is no longer a heretical world for the simple reason that heresy is disappearing. There are very few outside the Church today who believe in one tenth of the Christian doctrines taught by the so-called reformers of the sixteenth century. It takes a branch cut off from the vine some time to die, but it eventually dies. The branch is now dead, it exists only as a vague name to cover any "ism" from Humanism to Freudianism. The Catholic is no longer engaged in a Civil War, i.e., in conflict with Christian sects; rather he is resisting an invasion — the invasion of a secular philosophy of life. The problem of the future is not which is the true Church: but what is the nature of society? Is society to be organized on a technical or secular basis, or on a spiritual and eternal basis? Is society a God, or is it to worship God? Does God derive His authority from Caesar or does Caesar derive his authority from God?

The future battle will be between the Church and Communism. Communism itself admits that it has only one enemy and that is the Catholic Church. If it be objected that the influence of Communism is exaggerated it is well to remember that Russia was saying a little over thirty years ago that Communism would never come, and that the absurd anti-human philosophy of Karl Marx could never be put into practice. Furthermore, the modern tendency to set up an absolute state, to deny personal rights such as the right of conscience and the right of private property, is in itself Communistic in principle, if not in fact. Never before in the whole history of Christianity has the State played such a role as it does today. The old Caesarism had a State religion, but its gods were distinct from the State. In the new State there is no God but the State. The distinction between rendering to Caesar the things that are Caesar's and to God the things that are God's no longer holds. Caesar and God are identical. There is no God but the State.

This new State Absolutism is the basis of the crisis of this new era. A crisis arises whenever certain fundamental principles, according to which civilization has lived its social, political, and economic life, are challenged. Now, it is a fact that the modern world is challenging the principles according to which it has been living during the past four hundred years; namely, the principle of individualism, or the isolation of man from society.

Individualism had two consequences: *isolation* and *indifference.* The first effect was to isolate man from society, that is, it set up primacy of the individual as against the social, and denied that any organic society, such as the State or the Church, had any right to suggest how a man should conduct either his life or his business. As a matter of fact, any suggestion was looked upon as an interference with individual rights. If individuals did come together to form an organization, they produced merely something mechanical like a pile of bricks, but not anything organic like a body. An individual felt free to withdraw himself from society, provided society did not measure up to his wishes, very much as nations today withdraw themselves from the League of Nations if it does not do their bidding. The net result of this isolation from society was a kind of competitive individualism in which each man became a wolf to his neighbor. These were the days when so-called great leaders glorified "rugged individualism." The State had no other function than to keep others from meddling in economic affairs, with no regard to social control, or the good of the commonwealth, or much less to the glory of God. By appealing to individual rights, big business thus immunized itself to a great extent against all interference by the State, and succeeded in condemning collective bargaining by pleading for the right of an individual to make his own contract. The real reason was that big business knew it could control wages as long as it dealt with individuals, but could not do so if it dealt with groups. Over fifty years ago, Leo XIII protested against such economic individualism by pleading for collective bargaining for the sake of a living wage.

The second effect of individualism was indifference or a denial of a common truth. If every individual was free to believe and to do whatever he pleased, some scheme had to be devised which would allow conflicting views to coexist. Indifference to truth was the answer. A common truth, to which all men might appeal, as they appeal to the multiplication table, was denied. The most desirable spirit a man could possess was the spirit of "broadmindedness" which meant indifference to right or wrong, good and evil. The result was that any man who could make up his mind and dedicate himself wholeheartedly to a principle, was called narrow and a bigot, while the man who could never make up his mind and who changed his principles as he changed his clothes, was called broad and tolerant. It was under such a spirit that the Church was attacked as being behind the times, because she refused to surrender the immutable truths of Christ.

Now we come to the reason why there is a crisis in modern civilization. It was said that a crisis arose when certain basic principles were challenged. We have a crisis now because the principle of individualism, which has guided philosophy, religion, politics, and economics, is now challenged and denied. From the extreme error of Individualism, the world has swung to the opposite extreme of Collectivism. The word

Collectivism is here used to cover the new social movement which insists on the collectivity, the mass, the social, and the State, to the extent of crushing individuality. The reaction was rather natural. Individualism is selfishness; selfishness is power; power tends to dictatorship, and dictatorship means often the extinction of the individuals in the class, as the Holy Father Pius XI put it: "The accumulation of power, the characteristic note of the modern economic order, is the natural result of limitless free competition which permits the survival of those only who are strongest." Collectivism is thus not only a protest against individualism but also a development from it.

This collectivism has manifested itself in some countries in the collectivist policy of government regulation of business; in others, it worked itself out in Totalitarianism or the Absolute State, which was condemned in 1864 by Pius IX in his *Syllabus of Errors:* "The State as the fount and origin of all rights itself enjoys a right which knows no limit." It must not be thought that Russia is the only country which has denied the personal in man. Communism and the Totalitarian State are broader than Russia. The emphasis on the collectivity in the United States has taken on the form of refusing to allow labor and capital to work out their own solution apart from the social order. This stressing of the social rather than the economic has left untouched private property and religion. The Russian Collectivism destroyed both. In

Mexico, the Totalitarian State exists in something like the Russian form, for the present constitution of Mexico states that: "Every person in the United States of Mexico, shall enjoy those rights which are given to him by the Constitution." This, of course, means that man has no rights which the State cannot take away. In Germany, the Totalitarian State worked out racially, something akin to what was effected economically in Russia. Italy is not an anti-God state nor anti-private property state, but agrees with totalitarianism in (a) dictatorship; (b) and the suppression of parties.

As regards the Totalitarian States of Germany and Mexico: John Eppstein observes: "Fascism and National Socialism share with the seculariat and socialist dictatorships the same intolerance of political opposition; the same detestation of minorities; the same denial of freedom to the Press, the State, the cinema and the wireless. The same insistence upon monopolizing the formation of the minds of children and adolescents."[1] In *theory* the Fascist creed leaves little independence for religion: "Nothing without the State, nothing against the State; nothing beyond the State." In *practice,* however, Italian Fascism has not denied the right of religion as an ally to be conciliated.

The consequences of the new extreme of Collec-

---

[1] "The Totalitarian State" in *Church and State* edited by Fr. Lattey. "The Italian Fascist State takes account of the Church as a living element in the national being, as a cultural and social asset which must be incorporated into the new system." — Christopher Dawson, *Religion and the Modern State,* p. 52.

tivism are the opposite to those of Individualism. Individualism, it was said, had the double effect of (1) isolating man from society and (2) of developing indifference. Collectivism on the contrary (a) absorbs man into the State and (b) develops in place of indifference an intolerance, not on behalf of the truths of God, but for the human systems of a dictator or a party.

Isolation has become absorption. Under Individualism the State was regarded as a kind of "policeman," to use the phrase of Christopher Dawson, but under Collectivism, the State is "nurse," in the sense that it takes over many of the functions which were previously considered personal and inalienable, and treats man as a child who did not know what was good for himself. Hence the mania for planning. In some States, it did not take on an extreme form, but where free competition did not effect a just distribution of wealth the State had to step in and equivalently say: "If your individual conscience refuses to do what is morally just, then I, the State shall step in and by my power force you to do what is legally just." In other countries, coercive interference by the State did not achieve its desired result; in some countries the State socialized business; in others it nationalized business; while in others it set itself boldly to the radical task of turning over all ownership to the State, and this mobilization of property has ended in an error as bad; namely, State capitalism.

At one time we had wealth in the hands of a few; the new tendency is to concentrate wealth in the hands of the State. This is no solution of the social problem. This State absolutism has become such a nurse of the people that it has not only taken over their property, it has even taken over their souls. It possesses man from the cradle to the grave, by denying that he has any end and purpose other than the service of the State. Hence the elimination of the unfit, sterilization, birth-control clinics, all of which implicitly teach that man is the tool of the State and has no rights beyond the State; hence the tendency of the State to take over the functions of religion, and substitute a worship of the State for the worship of God, as is done in Russia, in Mexico, and to some extent in Germany; hence the movement to allow psychology to take the place of theology, psychoanalysis to take the place of a confessor, cures to take the place of penance, teachers to take the place of the clergy, and clinics to take the place of the Church. The result is that in the new society the living God becomes a kind of God Emeritus, very much like the retired rector of a university, retaining the empty title, but not permitted to exercise any claim to respect or love. Thus it is that man who was once free to do anything, is now free to do nothing; man who once was so individual that he could worship any God he wished is now mechanized and depersonalized until he has no more individuality than a pea in a pod; and he who could say the State existed for him, now finds that he exists solely for the State.

The second contrasting consequence of the new State is the emphasis on a common belief. Indifference to truth was the principal dogma of individualism. Submission to a creed as the State understands it, is the principal dogma of the new Totalitarianism. Under Individualism a man was free to decide his own morality and his own religion; under the new State man is not permitted to decide his own religion nor his own morality, for there is no conscience except State-conscience, no religion except State-religion, no morality but State-morality, and no God but the State. Hence the new States, such as Russia, have their State catechism, they persecute heretics, and they have their inquisitions which punish those who do not accept State beliefs. The result is that the world which once condemned the Church for being too dogmatic is now subject, not to dogmas which make it free, but dogmas which enslave. A new intolerance has taken the place of the old indifference — not the intolerance of Truth but the intolerance of a human system or a State economic.

In the first ages of the Church, persecution came from the outside; namely, from the pagans; later on, persecutions came from the inside; namely, from the heretics; today there is no external persecution by pagans, there is no internal persecution by heretics, rather religion and the Church today are denied and absorbed by the State which exists as a political society built on the basis of religion, laying claim to the whole man, body and soul, aping religion in the secular order as a parrot apes the speech of man and as a monkey apes his actions.

In summary, the modern world during the past four hundred years has witnessed two extreme solutions of the social problem, first, individualism which isolated man from society, like an arm amputated from a body, then came the other extreme of Collectivism which absorbs a man in society like an atom in a mass, a society in which all men are considered equal, because all men are equally slaves of the State. The position of the Church is a golden mean between these two extremes. She contends that the State is neither a collection of individuals isolated from organic relations with one another, nor a machine for the production of wealth, which is Communism, but a spiritual organism in which each person and class have functions to fulfill, and individual rights and duties in relation to the whole. Against Individualism the Church asserts that a man is a member of society in an organic way, as the eye and the ear, and the hand and the foot, are all members of the body. A man can no more live apart from society normally than an eye can live apart from the head. On the other hand, against Communism, she asserts that human personality has certain rights of which no State can deprive him. The heart, for example, is a member of the body, yet the heart has its own rights and functions in the body which the body itself cannot absorb. Man's inalienable and incommunicable rights are derived from the triune God in which each person of the Trinity is distinct from each other person. As Leo XIII stated in his encyclical *Immortale Dei,* "As the Almighty willed that in the heavenly kingdom itself the choirs of the angels should be of different ranks subordinated to one another; and as in the Church God has established different grades of orders with diversity of functions, so that all should not be apostles or doctors, nor all prophets, so also He has established a civil society of many orders of varying dignity, right, and power. And this to the end that the State like the Church should form one body comprising many members, some excelling others in rank and importance but all alike necessary to one another and solicitous for the common good.

"There is a certain orderly connection, which may be compared to the union of the soul and body in man. The nature and scope of that connection can be determined only, as we have laid down, by having regard to the nature of each power, and by taking account of the relative excellence and nobleness of their purpose. One of the two has for its proximate and chief object the well being of the mortal life; the other the everlasting joys of heaven. Whatever, therefore, in things human is of a sacred character, whatever belongs either of its own nature or by reason of the end to which it is referred, to the salvation of souls or to the worship of God, is subject to the power and judgment of the Church. Whatever is to be ranged under the civil and political order is rightly subject to the civil authority."

The Joint Pastoral Letter of the Bishops of the Netherlands issued in Lent, 1934, emphasized this truth specifically against the Totalitarian State: "Reason teaches us, and revelation confirms it, that man has certain rights. These rights are from nature, even apart from the State. The State does not create them and they do not derive merely from the purpose of the State, or from the interests of the nation but are bound up with the personal destiny of man. Because these rights precede all the regulations of the State, the State must respect them, even though they have to be regulated, that is, harmonized with the right of others. Undoubtedly, the good of the individual and the liberty it requires are subordinate to the common good: but they are not absorbed into it. The well-being of the whole is the well-being of *free personalities,* each with his own destiny. It would not be promoted but destroyed, were we to consider the State as the only source of rights, morality, and liberty. It is destroyed by every system which idolizes State and nation, and by every absolute dictatorship."

The proper concept of the State resides in the golden mean between Individualism which denies social control and Communism which denies personal liberty. The tendency today is toward the latter, or the Absolute, or Totalitarian, or Communistic State. Is this new tendency to emphasize the social, good or bad?

In theory, Collectivism when restricted to the economic order is not necessarily a greater evil than Individualism. Both are extreme solutions. The danger is that we may think the new concept wrong simply because it is a reaction against the old. It is well to remember, in this connection, that Leo XIII condemned the Liberalism and Individualism of the past century. Consequently, "there is no fundamental reason why the passing of parliamentary democracy and economic individualism should be opposed to Christian principles or sentiment. It is at least theoretically possible that the limitation of political and economic freedom by the extension of social control should be actually favorable to the cause of spiritual freedom."[2]

It may well be that the tendency toward dictatorship in the new State is the world's admission of the need of authority, and the emphasis on the social is a reassertion of the forgotten Christian principle of the solidarity of the human race; it may also be that the collectivism is a remedy for the failure of parliamentary forms of government to achieve their end. But Collectivism, in theory, is wrong when it denies the personal and inalienable rights of man.

But *in fact* the new State is not always respectful of

----

[2] C. Dawson, *Religion and the Modern State*, p. 51.

the true nature of man. And here mention must be made particularly of Mexico, Russia, and Germany, where the chalice of Gethsemane has been generously dipped to faithful souls. In all these countries the State is organized on a purely secular basis, and has set itself up as a counter-Church, crushing religion by the sheer force of State-power. It is not indifferent to religion as was the Liberal State; it is not only hostile to it as was the pagan State; but it is *hostile* and *possessive*. It not only crushes the Church but it takes over its functions, reduces the spiritual to the political, and gives the kingdom of anti-Christ a definite political form and social substance.[3] The conflict of the future in these States is between a society which recognizes God, and a society which calls itself God.

The Church has already come into conflict with the State in these countries. She says to the State: "I will render to Caesar the things that are Caesar's, but I insist on being allowed to render to God the things that are God's." The State, on the contrary, says to the Church: "We insist that you render unto Caesar even the things that are God's." The issue is very much like that which brought our Lord before Pilate. The charges preferred against Him were three: "We have found this man perverting our nation and refusing to give tribute to Caesar and saying that He is Christ and King." Every word of it was a lie. He did not pervert the nation. Rather did He spiritualize it

---

[3] *Ibid.*

by lifting up weary souls to the blessedness of the Kingdom of God. He did not refuse to give tribute to Caesar, for He commanded that men render unto Caesar that which was Caesar's. He did not call Himself a political King, but a spiritual King, whose kingdom was not of this world.

These three charges sent our Lord to His cross. The Cross bore an inscription in three languages; Hebrew, Latin, and Greek, symbolic of the three civilizations of Jerusalem, Rome, and Athens. Christ was crucified by the State in the name of religion, in the name of law, and in the name of beauty. And the charge in all three was the same — He had called Himself a King. He was anti-State.

And these same charges which are urged against the Church today are the direct heirs of the lies urged in the courtroom of Pilate. The Church is unjustly accused of perverting the nation, because she asserts that there is no power in a nation except from above; she is accused of refusing to give tribute to the State, because she refuses to worship the State as a God; she is accused of calling herself a king, because she also serves the glorious Kingship of Christ.

To the Cross the Church is sentenced on the same false charges. Already three nations have crucified her. It is not the civilization of Rome, Athens, and Jerusalem, but the civilizations of Mexico, Russia, and Germany which would send her to her death. How much longer it will continue, only God knows. But when time ends what will be the Church's final battle? Who will be her last enemy? Who will lift the last hand against her? Who will erect her last Cross? The Creed gives the answer. Why, among the four judges, has the Creed retained only the name of Pilate? The answer seems to be that in the last and final battle at the end of the world, between the forces of good and evil, the Church will go to her death in exactly the same way that Christ went to His — *suffering under Pontius Pilate.*

Chapter IX

SEEKING FIRST THE KINGDOM OF GOD

DESPITE the unneighborly attitude of the modern State to the Father's house, the Father's house has a definite obligation to the State and to the world. The Church is not to do ambulance work for the social order, but to regenerate it; that economic reconstruction is conditioned upon spiritual regeneration; that the ideal of men is to "be good" rather than to "make good"; and finally that a civilization is not superior because it has more bathtubs and electric switches, deeper tunnels and taller buildings, more automobiles and radios than any other civilization, but that it is superior if it produces better men and more saints. Civilization is not to be identified with commercial prestige but with moral worth; not with goods, but with goodness. It is just such false associations as these which forced our civilization to pay a price which it can ill afford to pay; namely, the spiritual alienation of great minds, from the truths of Christianity. Our age has as many great minds as any other age, but the pity is, that the saving truths of Christ and His Church are unknown to them. It is precisely this alienation which has produced scientists who know not God, kings who know not the King of kings, and international diplomats who know not the Prince of peace.

This does not mean that economics and politics and social theories are unimportant, for never before were they so important. This does not mean the Christian should not interest himself in these matters, for the Holy Father has explicitly stated: that Catholics must take an interest in politics, when "by politics is meant the common good in opposition to individual and particular goods"; but it does mean that the world must develop a sense of values. It must consider what is of primary and secondary importance, and realize that a man's attitude toward God determines his attitude toward his fellow man.

It is not going to be an easy task to convince the world that its troubles are not primarily economic and political, but moral and religious, and that the business of the Church is not exclusively the business of making us rich. The Church is Christ, and therefore her attitude is His; namely, what might be called that of *political and economic relativity*. This means that it does not matter profoundly what your politics or your economics or your finances are, but it does matter how your soul stands in relation to God. Particular systems of politics and economics are really not fundamental. Civilization can be great under a monarchy or a parliament, under a democracy or under imperialism. Civilization can be good under New Deals or Old

Deals, gold standards or silver standards, but no civilization can be good unless it serves and loves God. Hence, to Satan who would have given Him all the political and economic kingdoms of earth, our Lord flung one word "begone"; to those who would trap Him into a dispute about conquered and conquering peoples He said: "Render unto Caesar the things that are Caesar's, and to God the things that are God's"; and to those who would make Him intervene in matters of money He asks: "Who hath appointed Me judge or divider over you?" "Consider the lilies of the field, how they grow; they labor not, neither do they spin. But I say to you that not even Solomon in all his glory was arrayed as one of these. And if the grass of the field, which is today, and tomorrow is cast into the oven, God doth so clothe: how much more you, O ye of little faith? Be not solicitous, therefore, saying, What shall we eat; or what shall we drink, or wherewith shall we be clothed? . . . For your Father knoweth that you have need of all these things." And when He did speak of economic goods He said: "After these things do the Gentiles seek."

Politics and economics have a place in civilization but they have not first place, and especially when man is on the wrong road: His words ring immortally true! "Seek ye, therefore, *first* the Kingdom of God and His Justice, and all these things shall be added unto you."

The same false notion about the Church and prosperity prevailed in Rome at the time of its decline. Alaric came to Rome about the beginning of the fifth century, forced open the Salarian gate and sacked the Capitol. The whole world was stirred by the fall of this mighty Cedar of Lebanus. Not since the invasion of Rome by the Gauls in 387 B.C. or for nearly eight hundred years, had the capitol been so threatened, invaded, and outraged. Rome felt she was invulnerable because eternal, little realizing that she was eternal not because of the force of her arms, but because a fisherman was to dwell there. Immediately the cry went up: "We have perished because we have become Christians. Christianity has failed us. We are not so powerful, we are not so mighty, we are not so great as we were with the gods of Olympus and the Forum. We are weak with the weakness of the God on a Cross Peter brought back from Calvary. Christianity has brought us bad luck."

St. Augustine in far-off Africa heard the cry and answered its challenge in his mighty work *The City of God*. He reminded the fallen empire that it had fallen not because it was Christian, but because it had failed to be Christian.

He admitted Rome had done great things for the world but these benefits had been purchased by slavery, and oppression of the weak, and in the end served only senseless luxury. He told them in no uncertain terms, that Christianity never promised to be a social panacea, *that the world was only a road and not a house* to live in, that life is a pilgrimage to another city, and not the art of making a heaven on earth,

that the benefits of Christianity are not material, but
spiritual, like His blood which regenerates us unto
life everlasting.

The world would not listen to Augustine. The
world then believed, as it believes now, that civilization is identical with economic progress, and that
Christianity fails when it fails to make the world prosperous. Within the Church as well as outside Augustine was begged to be quiet about Christianity bringing supernatural benefits. Everywhere men pleaded:
"Si taceat de Roma — If he would only shut up about
Rome."* But he did not shut up. He preached and
cried down the error that the sole business of Christianity is business. And in this day and age when
Catholics remind the world that its economics and
politics are not nearly so important as its morals and
its religion, that its social structure cannot be made
right until men make their peace with God, and that
society cannot be improved except by reforming the
individuals who make it,[1] the cry of Augustine's day

---

[1] "Till we look at home, no good shall we be able to perform for
the Church at large; we shall but do mischief, when we intend good,
and to us will apply that proverb — 'Physician heal thyself.' Let us learn
first to 'come' diligently 'to the waters,' and ask for that gift of God,
which will be 'a well of water in us springing up unto everlasting life.'
And let us not doubt that if we do thus proceed, we shall advance the
cause of Christ in the world, whether we see it or not, whether we will
it or not, whether the world wills it or not. Let us raise the level of
religion in our hearts, and it will rise in the world. He who attempts
to set up God's kingdom in his heart, furthers it in the world." —
Cardinal Newman, Sermons: Subjects of the Day, Sermon X, pp. 133, 134.

is hurled in their faces: *"O si taceat de Roma!* — Oh, if he would only shut up about Rome, about the sanctity of marriage, about education built upon Christ, about grace, about the sacraments and eternal life." But in these days as in the days of Augustine there must be no silence. Spiritual regeneration must condition social reconstruction. There is no other way than the way of the Lord. He, the living Bread, came on earth when there was a famine and was born in a little city called Bethlehem, the House of Bread. He came on earth when armies were great and powerful and said that he who took the sword would perish by the sword; He came at a time when slaves were ill treated and yet preached, "servants obey your Master"; He came on earth when men would have proclaimed Him King of their economics and politics and said: "My Kingdom is not of this World"; He came on earth to a people who hated Caesar as their unjust oppressor and said: "Render to Caesar the things that are Caesar's, and to God the things that are God's." He came on earth when men judged Him by His earthly power and said: "Take up your cross and follow Me."

The secularization of our culture, the enmity of the modern State need not make us despair. The Church makes its greatest progress when the present moment is discouraging and the future looks darkest. The world never seemed so close to victory as when it crucified Christ, and yet that was the day of its

defeat. Christ never seemed less like a King, less a
world Conqueror than the day when they gave the
King a crown of thorns, and the Conqueror the throne
of a Cross. And yet on that black day we have since
called Good Friday, He won His greatest victory.

So it is with the Church. It is weak when it is
strong with the power of the world; but it is strong
when it appears to be weak in the eyes of men. The
reason is that the real forces which conquer are not
the forces of wealth, machinery, and politics, but the
spiritual forces, and above all the Spirit of the Sacrifice
on Calvary which rises to its Easter after the ignominy
of a Good Friday. Thus the Church in its history is
constantly undergoing Resurrections, like the seed in
the springtime; always being left as dead in a tomb,
and yet always walking in the newness of life. It is
born again for each new age to save the age. At this
moment she seems to be living in a Good Friday, and
Christ her Spouse is dipping the Chalice of His sorrow
to her first in this country, and then in that, but all
for the holy purpose of perfecting her for the Divine
Harvest which lies in the immediate future.

The precise way in which this regeneration is to
take place is by a revival of the Pentecostal ideal. It
was by the Pentecostal spirit the world was renovated
in the first century, and it is the way it will be renovated in the twentieth. And what is the Pentecostal
ideal? It is the recognition of the primacy of the spiritual, inspired by an abundant outpouring of the

Spirit upon the souls of men, and by a stirring up of the grace of Confirmation. The Pentecostal ideal means that men first contemplate,[2] then actuate; that they live by loves, and not by cupidities; and that they

----

[2] "Contemplation is the indispensable and the informing spirit of every organic society. It alone can apprehend the form. It maintains the social form of a society that is both free and organic. And the more adequate the contemplation, that is, the more adequate the social form it perceives and expresses, the better is the society which contemplates and embodies this social form. A society lacking social contemplation of truth and an organic social form as its embodiment, is really an inorganic society held together merely by making the conflicting interests conform, not an organic whole, all of whose parts are organs of a life, which regulates their activities in the realization of a form.

"The fact that all intellectual achievement, even the culture of humanity are fruits of the contemplative class, is proof enough for the primacy of contemplation. The breaking up of the older European societies was due to misplaced values, which contemplation should have discovered and condemned. Sacrificing the supreme value of religious truth, and that of freedom of conscience to the lower value of national unity are violations of the order of values as manifest in contemplation.

"Our present-day perversions of the order of contemplation are closely linked with the great social disorder. A society which smothers religion, which worships applied science, and which makes the machine the master instead of the servant of mankind, is guilty of gross injustice. We blame Bolshevik Russia for her subversion of values which ranks productive labor as the highest form of human activity, and subordinates man's thought and very life to the sheer acquisition of economic goods — all to the downright contempt of the order of spirit. However, it should be different today. When applied science has produced wealth unparalleled in human history, and when the machine has reached an enormous productive capacity, we should expect that many could realize leisure for contemplation. The ultimate function of machinery should be none other than to make time for contemplation for the masses, that they may be provided for as were the few of the Roman Empire by the slave system. Pure activism unless it be supported by contemplation, ends in disaster." — E. I. Watkin, *A Philosophy of Form,* p. 164 ff. (New York: Sheed and Ward).

love without losing their hearts. The Pentecostal ideal insists that social amelioration is a *by-product* of Christianity. The important word here is "by-product" in the sense that the Church does not directly set out to make the world economically and politically prosperous, but only secondarily. The prime purpose is to make men serve the Kingdom of God and His Justice, and all these other things will be added unto her.

There is always a great social and political catastrophe wherever there is a decline of Pentecostal spirit. The Prophet of old had warned his day: "Peace, peace and there is no peace because no man considereth in his heart." History reveals that in England between the years 1399 and 1509 there were only eight religious houses opened in England. Anyone who knew the importance of the spiritual life in the life of a nation, knew that something was going to crack, and what did crack was the religious unity of England, which has not since been recovered.

This Pentecostal ideal, it has recently been pointed out, has manifested itself in various ways at various periods of history, for the ways of God are many and mysterious. At the beginning of the Church's history, the ideal manifested itself in asceticism, when men and women withdrew themselves from the corrupt pagan civilization of their times and retired into the desert. They felt there was no possible compromise with the secular pagan atmosphere, and hence the best way to live the Christian life and to fulfill the

Pentecostal inspiration was to live isolated from the world.

When the Middle Ages began to flourish, the Pentecostal ideal manifested itself in the monastic life, wherein great corporate bodies like the Franciscans and Dominicans were formed in the midst of society which was no longer inimical to spiritual interests, but capable of being impregnated by it. It was in these days that the social, political, and economic life of the people became more infused with the spiritual life than at any other period of the world's history.

Later in the Reformation period, the Pentecostal spirit took on a new form. No longer was it apart from corrupt society, as it was in the days of the Fathers of the Desert; no longer was it the soul of civilization, as it was in the Middle Ages; it was now called upon to fight for the Pentecostal truths which were denied in the hour of moral laxity. In those days the Pentecostal ideal manifested itself not only in the individual champions of Faith like Bossuet, but also in societies like the Jesuits which began a militant crusade against error armed with the sword of truth.

We are at a new crisis of the world's history. What form will the Pentecostal spirit take now? Will it demand retirement from the world, will it raise up new monastic bodies, will it raise up new champions of the truth? We know not what God has in store for us. We know only that we shall not perish. But there does seem to be more indication of the form the Pentecostal

spirit will take in the future; namely, the one suggested by the Vicar of Christ: Catholic Action. The
layman is coming into his own. The Sacrament of
Confirmation will soon be recognized with even
greater clarity as the sacrament of lay action.

The term *Catholic Action* is vague, as it is presently used, but that is because we too often speak of it
apart from the Mystical Body of the Church. Catholic
Action is based on the principle that Catholicism is
an abstract term, and is operative and functional only
by and through Catholics themselves. Catholic Action
reminds the laity that while the Church is the bearer
of the life of humanity, it is through the members
themselves that this life is communicated to humanity.
All the tragedies of Catholicism arise from the failure
of individual Catholics to rise to their opportunities
and to permeate their social and intellectual environment with their faith. Catholic Action means that
from this point on, the Church must be operative not
only through the bishops and priests who govern it,
but through the laity who are engaged in even the
most trivial of the world's activities.

In the Mystical Body, one member cannot dispense
with another member any more than the hand can say
to the foot. "I can dispense with your services." This
is because the Church is made up of a multiplicity of
members as the body is formed of a multiplicity of
cells. The Church fails in those parts where its members fail. Hence the importance of each member of

the Church doing the work assigned to him, in his
particular state of life. Catholic Action means precisely
this; it does not mean that a hand should be a foot,
but that the hand should be a good hand, and the
foot a good foot. This idea can be clarified by recall-
ing that the Holy Father recognizes as an ideal in the
conversion of pagan peoples, not the apostolate of
foreign missionaries among them, but the developing
of native apostles, so that the Japanese may be converted by the Japanese, the Chinese by the Chinese,
and so forth. This is also the ideal of Catholic Action.
Too often we think of Catholic Action as zealous lay-
men going into "foreign" fields to evangelize them,
for example, doctors laboring to purify the stage,
lawyers working to spiritualize the trade unions. Catholic Action does not mean this *in ideal*. It means, if
we follow the theology of the Holy Father, that the
different groups and classes will be Catholicized by
and through the Catholics *in those groups,* i.e., that
the stage will be cleansed by and through Catholics
on the stage; the medical profession will become
ethical by and through Catholic doctors; law will be
made honest by and through Catholic lawyers; working classes will be saved from Communism for the
communion of saints, by and through Catholic workers themselves. The bishop labors in his diocese, the
priest in his parish, and the layman in his trade, and
if every Catholic played his role well in his particular
profession, they would soon "succeed in bringing

about a common peace amongst men, by devoting all their energies to the propagation and restoration of the Kingdom of Christ."[3]

The Church is the Mystical Body of Christ. Each Catholic, therefore, in his little world is Christ. Our Lord has no other feet with which to go about doing good, than ours; He has no other cheeks to turn to those who preach class warfare, than our own; He has no other lips with which to teach those who sit in the superstition of the Gentiles, than our own. Christ fails in the measure we fail to be Christ-like. No one is unimportant; no action is a-moral or a-Catholic; everything and everyone is impregnated with spiritual significance. Never before has the world been so willing to accept spiritual influence; seldom since the Incarnation have the average man and woman, oppressed with a sense of false values and ambiguous standards, been so disposed to receive spiritual guidance. And the way they are to be infused is through Catholic Action, or the working of the Pentecostal spirit through every influential cell of the Mystical Body — the leaven of the world.

Spirituality. The world crisis can be healed only by forces not directly involved in the crisis itself. A sick man, for example, must rely on medicine for his cure; a ship must anchor outside itself, an eagle can fly only by the aid of something non-eagle; namely, the air. In like manner, modern civilization cannot lift

----

[3] Pius XI, *Ubi Arcano Dei.*

itself out of the chaos by the bootstraps of the economic and the political, but only by a power other
than the political and the economic and therefore
something not directly involved in its ruin. Important
as the political and the economic are, it is still more
important to hearken back to our Lord's plan of social
reconstruction through spiritual regeneration. His
method was to make economic and social justice the
by-product of Christian living. He reminds us that a
purely secular civilization cannot save itself, because
natural man has not sufficient moral strength to sacrifice himself for the common good. That is why He
saved the world by dying for it — to teach us that without Him and His Spirit of Sacrifice we could do nothing. That, too, is why He gathered unto Himself a
group of men whom He imbued with totally different
ideals than the world and radically different means to
attain those ideals. "I have chosen you out of the
world," He said; and He literally lifted them physi-
cally out of the world by putting them in a desert
place apart, and spiritually out of the world by infus-
ing them with a new spirit and the primacy of things
divine. "Seek ye therefore first the kingdom of God,
and His justice and all these things shall be added
unto you." When He had regenerated them and made
them new with the fires of His Spirit, He sent them
back again into the world — but they were no longer
the same men. They were different men.

That is why He said: "If the world hate you, know

ye that it hath hated Me before you. If you had been of the world, the world would love its own: but because you are not of the world, therefore the world hateth you." More than this, He told them they were to risk everything on His way of living, to be prepared to be hated by brother and sister, father and mother, to be dragged before magistrates and kings, and even to be led to death. There was to be no turning back, for no man putting his hand to the plow and looking back was fit for the Kingdom of God. The dead were to bury their dead, but they were to follow Him by taking up their cross daily, that is, by being prepared to lead an absolutely selfless life for the glory of God and the salvation of souls.

This wholehearted surrender to Christ is the only spirit which will conquer the world today, for the world is through accepting half-baked philosophies of life and milk-and-water religions. We are living in days of fire and blood when men want something that makes demands on them, and possesses both their bodies and their souls. Only enthusiastic apostles and zealous disciples who are willing to sacrifice and even to die will be heard in this day. That is why Communism is making an appeal; despite its enslaving materialism the men who preach it believe in it. They have taken the word "leaven" used by our Lord and changed it to "cell"; they have taken the word "mass" and changed it to "front." Burning with zeal for their cause, they ask for only a few men filled with the spirit of Marx and willing to sacrifice everything for that spirit, and with this "cell" they threaten to ferment and foment the whole "front." They say: "Give us three or four good Communists inspired with a hatred of Capitalism, with the doctrine of class struggle and the spirit of revolution, and let us put them into a labor union and we will communize the whole union. Give us three or four university professors who are on fire for the dialectics of materialism, and even though their students do not understand it, we will commuize the whole university." Such zeal can be met only with zeal, such courage only with courage, and such sacrifice only with sacrifice. No Liberal was ever willing to incommode himself for Liberalism, but Communists are very willing to sacrifice themselves for Communism. In this day of intense loyalties the sleek repose of Christians who will not sacrifice themselves for the things of God cannot meet the new challenge. It will take a great faith in Christ to put down faith in anti-Christ; it will take nothing less than the sacrifice of the Cross to conquer the sacrifice of those who crucify.

May it not be that God is, by the mysterious ways of His Providence, already sifting the wheat of apostolic souls from the chaff of the indifferent. As a matter of fact the purging has already gone on in some countries. God is, as it were, choosing disciples from the multitudes, and apostles from the disciples, and Peters and James and Johns from among the apostles. The

persecution of the Church in Mexico, in Russia, in
Spain, and in Germany has meant an increase and a
decrease — an increase in the quality of the Church,
and a decrease in quantity. Numbers mean little to the
Church, but spirituality means everything. It may very
well be, then, that God is preparing the Church for
the future battle or future peace by a spiritual purifi-
cation in which only the strong will walk with Him.
What was true in the days of Gideon is true in our
own day. Gideon, it will be recalled, battled the
Madianites whose army numbered 135,000 men.
Gideon asked if God would be with him and received
the sign through the sign of the fleece. Sounding the
trumpet, Gideon gathered an army of 32,000 men.
God told him his army was too large; the children of
Israel might think they conquered because of the
force of their arms, rather than the power of God.
Gideon then asked all fearful and timorous men to
leave, and 22,000 cowards left the ranks. But even that
army was too large, God told Gideon, and He bade
him take his army to the waters. All who lapped the
water in the hands after the fashion of men of action
were to be placed on one side of the river; those who
lay prone on the ground to drink at their ease were to
be put on the other side of the river. And of the 10,000
men only 300 lapped the water with their hands. With
that trivial army of only 300 men Gideon went out
and put to flight the army of 135,000 and Israel had
peace for forty years. The moral is that 300 zealous

souls who rely on God can do more than 32,000 indifferent ones who trust in their arms, and also that
no enemy is too great if God is with us.

It is difficult to convince our contemporaries of this
truth, that our ills are not only political and financial
but fundamentally moral and religious. They almost
identify the moral aspect of the problem with the impractical. Perhaps this analogy will help to impress
upon minds the primacy of the spiritual in matters
economic and political. Suppose America were conquered by a foreign power, whom, for the sake of
avoiding odious references we will call the Lenites.
Suppose a Lenite tetrarch was set up in Washington;
suppose our religion was called a "barbaric superstition"; suppose Lenite soldiers walked through our
streets, collected our taxes, and now and then induced
some American to work for them and collect taxes
from their fellow men; suppose the capital of the
United States was transferred to Lenopolis; suppose we
no longer had the right to coin our money; suppose
the judges of our courts had no power of life and death
over our citizens, but only a Lenite court could im-
pose death, and did so freely; suppose the Lenitians
regarded us as mentally and socially inferior, despite
the fact that we loved our independence and were
fond of our glorious history.

Now, suppose furthermore, the Incarnation had not
yet taken place, and our Lord was born in some in-

significant Bethlehem in America; and about the time we are speaking would have reached the middle of His Public Life. Now let me ask the question: In the midst of such financial, political, and economic woes what do you think would be the first question Americans would ask our Lord?

It would be without doubt: "Do you think it is lawful to pay tribute to Lenites?" Or in other words, "What do you think of the Lenitian question?" The economic and the political and not the need of purging ourselves would be uppermost in our minds. And how would our Lord have answered the question? Fortunately we need not speculate. We definitely know the answer, for the conditions described here are identically the same as our Lord met in Israel. Israel was conquered by the Romans in the year 63 B.C. Their capital was Rome; their religion was called by Cicero in his oration against Flaccus "an abominable superstition"; Roman soldiers policed their streets and induced some Jews to gather taxes for them; these Jews called "publicans," of which Matthew was one, were intensely hated by their fellow men. The Jews had not the power of coining money. It is recorded of one Rabbi that he so detested the payment of his tribute that during his whole lifetime he never looked upon the image of the emperor. The Jewish judges had no power of life and death — that is why Pilate and not Annas or Caiphas could condemn Christ to death. Finally, the Jews loved their great national history, but the Romans such as Tacitus spoke of them as an "abominable tribe."

Into such conditions our Lord was born. And what was the first question of importance to them: It was the political question; the financial question; the social question; the "What do you think of the Romans?" question. "Is it lawful to give tribute to Caesar?"

And how did our Lord answer it? "Bring me a penny that I may see it." The coin is handed to Him. "Whose is this image and inscription?" "Caesar's," they answered. Then He strikes. "Render therefore to Caesar the things that are Caesar's; and to God, the things that are God's." In other words, the important problem is not the Roman problem or the Lenite problem, but the spiritual problem: "Seek ye therefore first the kingdom of God, and His justice, and *all these things* will be added unto you." And so He left Caesar on his throne, Pilate on his judgment seat, Herod in his court, and sent out His Apostles full of the spirit of God and conquered a world

The social order we build will depend upon how we answer the question: What is the purpose of living? If life has no other goal than the dust, then we will build an order either of individual selfishness, which is Liberalism, or of collective selfishness, which is Communism; for if this life is all, why should we not have all? But if life is moral, and the way we live in charity, justice, peace, and sacrificing determines our existence in the next world, then what doth it profit if we gain the whole world and lose our immortal souls? These two philosophies of life are the Communistic and the Christian; one material, the other spiritual. Communists have only one word in their vocabulary and that is the word *Down* — "Down with Capitalism! Down with the Rich! Down with the bourgeoisie! Down with the Wealthy! Down with Governments! Down with Classes! Down with Religion! Down with God!"

Heavens above! Is there not another word in our vocabulary upon which we can build a true social order? Can one build anything *down?* Must not everything that is built be built upward? Let there be another order constructed upon the word *Up!* Up from Class-struggle! Up from Hate! Up from Revolution! Up from the material! Up from the dust! Up beyond the earth, beyond the stars, up to the "hid battlements of eternity" — Up — Up to **God!**

Chapter X

OUR OPPORTUNITY AND OUR
RESPONSIBILITY

THERE is always a temptation to lay the flattering unction to our souls that we have done our Christian duty when we have poured our vials of righteous wrath upon the godless, and denounced Communism as the monstrous red enemy of man. Such an attitude makes us like other Pharisees who feel justified in throwing stones because we have found the adulteress.

The point we wish to make now is that this view is wrong and unbecoming a Catholic. It is wrong because we have been sent into this world not to condemn the wrong, but to make the wrong right; not to cry "unclean" but to wash clean; not to damn but to save. As followers of our Lord we must never forget "they that are in health need not a physician, but they that are ill," and that He came into the world "not to call the just but sinners." This means very definitely that it is not our business to prove they are wrong, however satisfying it may be; it is not even our business to prove we are right, as if the truth were our

making, and not God's. It is our business to preach
Christ and Him Crucified and let that Truth conquer
by its own right. When a man is starving you need
not go to him and say: "You must not eat poisons.
Poisons will kill you!" You need not even say: "You
must eat bread. Science has proved that there are
vitamins in bread." You need only go to him and say:
"You are hungry; here is bread," and the laws of nature will do the rest. And so it is with starving souls.
We need not reprove their error, nor show *we* are
right, but present the truth of God and with the help
of His grace it will nourish them unto Life everlasting.

Taking this point of view, how should we approach
atheists and bigots How should we deal with Communists who are spreading doctrines so disruptive of
family life, property, culture, and peace? How did our
Lord and St. Paul deal with those who practiced Communistic principles in their day, even though they
were not called Communists? They converted souls
by finding a common denominator between them and
the truth they preached.

Take the case of the woman at the well. Our Lord,
weary from His journey on a hot summer day said to
her: "Give Me to drink." She immediately reminded
Him that the well was deep and He had nothing
wherein to draw. Our Lord said to her: "If thou didst
know the gift of God, and who he is that saith to thee
'Give Me to drink' thou perhaps wouldst have asked
of Him, and He would have given thee living water."

And that poor woman who daily had trudged out from Samaria in the boiling sun with the waterpot upon her head, was most anxious to find a source of living water which would dispense her from future journeys. But our Lord, seeing she did not understand His spiritual message, changed the subject. "Go call thy husband." The woman answered "I have no husband." Jesus said to her: "Thou hast said well: 'I have no husband,' for thou hast had five husbands; and he whom thou hast, is not thy husband."

Now what possible basis of apostleship could there be between our Lord who is Innocence itself, and this adulterous woman with five husbands? There was only one common denominator and that was a common love of a drink of cold water, and from that common starting point our Lord drew the sinner on to an understanding of grace and the supernatural life, and such an understanding it was, that she and her fellow townspeople of the despised city were the first in history to address Him as "the Saviour of the world."

The tactics of St. Paul in Athens were like those of His Master at Jacob's well. St. Paul's spirit was stirred at "seeing the city wholly given to idolatry." He knew they had their gods on the Olympic heights; he knew that they had a god for every household; he knew they had gods Aeneas brought from Troy, but he sought about for a common denominator, and he found it in a word — the word, *Unknown.* "Standing in the midst of the Areopagus, he said: 'Ye men of Athens, I perceive that in all things you are too superstitious. For passing by, and seeing your idols I found an altar also on which was written: "To the Unknown God." What therefore you worship without knowing it, that I preach to you: God who made the world.' " From that common denominator of the word *unknown* we might also say from a pun — St. Paul led them on to the knowledge of the true God in whom we move and have our being. As our Lord in conversation with the women did not spend all His time denouncing adultery, as much as He detested it, so neither did St. Paul before the Aeropagus spend all his time denouncing idolatry as much as he abhorred it; both sought about for one trivial common thing which Christianity had with sin and idolatry, and through that common denominator led souls on to the fullness of the light.

And so it is with us — We must not spend our energies denouncing Communism; we are to lead Communists into the camp of the Communionists by finding some common denominator with them, even though it be as low as a common love of water, or a common search for the great unknown.

In that search for a common denominator, one spirit above all others must prevail, and that is the spirit of Christ-like charity. We must be intolerant about Communism, and atheism, but tolerant to Communists and atheists. If we had the same education they had, if we had been fed upon the same Marxian lies and half truths about religion as they have, we would probably hate the Church ten times more than they do. They do not really hate the Church; they only hate what they have been taught about the Church. We would burn churches, too, if we had been falsely trained to believe that the Church stood for the very social injustices they rightly condemn. Our Lord found an excuse for them on Calvary; can we do less by echoing in our lives "Father, forgive them for they know not what they do."

The saints of the Church have always been fond of repeating that we could catch more flies with a drop of honey, than with a barrel of vinegar. St. Vincent de Paul in particular has cautioned us: "A man is not believed because he is clever, but because he is liked and known to be good. The devil is very clever, and we don't believe a word he says, because we don't like him. Nobody will believe us unless we are loving and forebearing with them." As it has been repeated many times: "In necessary things there must be agreement and unity; in doubtful or indifferent things there must be charity — giving no offense to any man that our ministry be not blamed." And this lesson of charity the Holy Father has set for us when he asked that the prayers after Low Mass be said for the persecuted Russians, ninety-nine per cent of whom are not in communion with the Holy See.

Grant that Communists and atheists and bigots do hate Christ and His Church. They do not hate Plato nor an Oriental sun-cult. Is not this because only an infinite object can be infinitely hated and infinitely loved, and also because their hatred is but a vain attempt to despise? But all that hate does not dispense us from praying for them as our Lord prayed for His executioners, and Stephen interceded for those who stoned him. It is well to remember that hateful souls can be transformed in the fire of God's grace into loving souls. Our Lord chose His greatest Apostles from the weak and the hateful and the sinful! Peter from weakness; Paul from hate; and Magdalene, who has oft been called the thirteenth Apostle, from voluptuousness. Our Lord died for each and every one of them; hence we must see in them not men to be hated, but potential captives of the Man on the Cross who died out of love — even for Stalin.

Russia is the home of godlessness, but Russia could just as well have the mission to Christianize modern Europe as to give it anti-Christ. Its history has been full of a Messianic consciousness that it was destined to give something to the world, and its present pains could just as well be the pangs of birth as the groan of death. God in His Mercy often raises up individuals from great sins, such as Augustine, that they might declare forth the power of His Love, for those who have been at death's door can best reveal the glories of health. Why could not God not only raise up individuals, but even nations, from the darkness of hate to the light of love, so that they might be as examples of His Mercy and Apostles of His Truth to them that

sit in the superstition of the Gentiles? Why could there
not be social Magdalenes, and social Pauls as well as
individual Magdalenes and individual Pauls? No nation is too far gone as yet to consider it beyond redemption. As the Holy Father has told us: "Beneath
the embers there still are to be found sparks that can
be fanned into flame." England, for example, seemed
hopeless to the faith in the days of Queen Elizabeth
when she murdered one hundred and thirty-eight
secular priest, six Jesuits, one Benedictine, and one
Franciscan; it seemed even hopeless in 1834 with
only four bishops and 400,000 faithful, and yet today
it has twenty-seven bishops and over three million
faithful. What is true of England in the past can be
true of Communistic Russia and anticlerical Mexico.
They are not beyond redemption, for they are only
wounded, not lost. This is not a black, dark, dreadful,
and hateful world bound for the precipice of destruction; it is a world of infinite possibilities. It is not a
lost world! It can still be saved, but saved only by the
Charity of God living in souls who are ready if need
be to come out of other Catacombs to save it!

Too long has the world lived on the assumption
that religion is a private affair. Now it has learned
that by regarding it as such, irreligion has pre-empted
the entire social order. It will no longer do for individuals to preach about the necessity of personal piety
alone, for our lives are inextricably entangled with
all the problems of civilization. There is not one kind

of spirituality for man, and another for society; there is only one for both, for the power that builds the soul is the power that builds the world. The Kingdom of God, it is true, is not *of* this world, but as long as time endures, it is *for* this world. We therefore have not only a vocation to sanctify and save our souls, but also to expand and diffuse that sanctification to save society. The very prayers we say suggest that we are related to a great social pattern as the cells of a body are related one to another: We say "Our Father," not "My Father"; we ask: "Forgive us our trespasses" not "Forgive me my trespasses"; we are commanded to "love God and our neighbor, and our enemies, and to pray for our executioners." The Church itself is the leaven in the mass which ferments the whole, the city on the hill; the light of the world to illumine the darkness. Religion, then, is not an individual affair; it is social. We do not save ourselves alone, but only in conjunction with others. Such is the meaning of the divine reminder: "You are the salt of the earth, and if the salt lose its savor, wherewith shall it be salted."

Quite apart from this divine injunction there is still another reason for our responsibility toward the modern world and its chaos, and that is that chaos is partly of our own making. If we are honest with ourselves, we cannot deny that the advance of secularism, the increase of godlessness, the decline of the sacrificial spirit, is to a small extent at least, a result of our own unfulfilled Christian duty, a failure to live out in our social and economic and political existences, the fullest implication of the cross that was signed on our backs the day of our baptism, and on our foreheads the hour of our confirmation. The very fact that the world is a thousand times more scandalized at a bad Catholic in public life than a bad anything else, is only a proof that the world expected much more of him. To just that extent that we have colored our Christian outlook on life with the veneer of worldliness or have tried to make the best of two worlds, or have used our faith only as a consolation and the world as our luxury, or failed to radiate the light of God's Truth to those who walk in darkness — to just that extent, the guilt of the world's sin is on our hands and its responsibility on our souls. Human perversity, diabolical propaganda, vicious lies, unchained concupiscences, passion, envy, and love of power — all these have done much to upset the world, but there is no doubt that it would be less upset, if we had risen to the full consciousness of what it means to be a Christian. We make the world by living our faith; we unmake it by falling short of it. We save the world by loving the cross; we lose it by fleeing even from its shadows.

If then, the chaos of civilization is partly the result of our compromise with the cross, it follows that we have an obligation to make reparation for it, and this can be done only by a renewed sense of responsibility and apostleship to the world in general and to two groups in particular: *marginal Christians* and the *masses.*

By marginal Christians is meant those on the fringe of religion who are descendants of Christian-living parents but who now are Christians only in name, retaining a few of its ideals out of indolence and force of habit. They know Christianity only through certain emasculated forms of it which married the spirit of the age and are now dying with it. Of Catholicism, its Sacraments, its pardon, its grace, its certitude, and its peace, they know nothing except a few inherited prejudices. And yet they are good people who want to do the right thing, but who have no definite philosophy concerning it. They educate their children without religion, and yet resent their compromising morals. They feel that Bertrand Russell is right in his attack on authority, and yet they bemoan their children's disobedience. They would be angry if you told them they were not Christian, and yet they do not believe that Christ is God; on the other hand, they resent being called pagan, for they do like hymns and they want their daughters to have a church wedding. There is only one thing of which they are certain and that is that things are not right as they are. It is just that single certitude which makes them what might be called the great "potential," for they are ready to be pulled in either of two directions.

That immediately creates the problem: What is going to happen to this group when the challenge is hurled and the crisis arrives? Within a very short time, they must take sides; they must either gather with

Christ or they must scatter; they must either be with Him or against Him; they must either be on the cross as other Christs, or under it as other executioners. There was a middle course a few years ago, but there is one no longer. Communism has done away with all the halfway houses; it has brought the world face to face with fundamentals; it has cleared the issues by reminding the world there are only two philosophies of life: Communism which mobilizes souls for secular ends and dust; and Christianity which sanctifies them for eternal ends and God. Which way then will these marginal Christians tend? Will they turn right, which in Christian language is upward to the God of Love for whom they were made, or will they turn left, which is downward to class-struggle and the destiny of animals? The answer depends upon those who have the Faith. Like the multitudes who followed our Lord into the desert, they are as sheep without a Shepherd. They are waiting to be shepherded either with the sheep or goats. Only this much is certain. Being human and having hearts they want more than class-struggle and economics; they want Life, they want Truth, and they want Love. In a word, they want Christ. That is why the advantage is on our side, for it is ours to give them Christ. If they receive Him not, it will be only because we have failed.

We have responsibility not only toward marginal Christians but also toward the *masses* — what Communists call the proletariat, the Capitalists call labor, governments call the unemployed, and social agencies call the maladjusted, and what we must call potential children of the Kingdom of God. This group has so long been the victim of social injustices that it feels any force which will ameliorate their economic lot is necessarily their savior. Communism, knowing that souls can be bought for thirty pieces of silver, immediately presents itself as their champion and the great enemy of social injustices. And the significance of Communism and the power of its appeal cannot be minimized. Communism is right in its *protests:* the masses do have too many wants and too few rights. But it is wrong in its *reforms.* It falsely leads the masses to believe they have only stomachs, as Capitalism falsely led them to believe they had only hands. Who will get to the masses first? Will it be Communism mobilizing them into a revolutionary force, or Catholicism uniting them into a moral force? The answer depends on how seriously we take our faith. It is here that our responsibility begins; namely, to feed not only their stomachs and busy their hands, but also to teach them they have souls as well as bodies, that the happiness of a man consists not in what he has, but in what he is, not in the quantity of his possessions, but how he uses them. It is our solemn duty to go down to them and build up just as strong, just as vigorous a Christian proletariat as others would build up a Communistic proletariat. It is our duty not alone because they are unemployed, not alone because they are victims of social injustice, but because they are poor, and the poor in spirit are the stuff from which the future civilization will be built. The influences making for the new era will come *not from above, but from below,* not from individuals with wealth, but from groups with holy purposes, not from the well-to-do, but from the will-to-reform. The Church itself even more than civilization will draw its strength from them, as our Lord drew His Apostles from them. By their very nature they possess a power of cohesion which the rich often lack, for wealth without religion breeds false distinctions and snobbery. They possess a natural solidarity which can easily be woven into the supernatural unity of the Mystical Body of Christ. In Spain, in Russia, in Mexico, they have, in frenzies of indignation, burned churches, but this is because they were told the Church was against them. The Church that was born of the Poor Man of Galilee cannot tolerate this lie! It is not enough for us to shout it down. The shouts cannot be heard amid burning embers and falling steeples. It must be *lived down,* and it can be lived down only by Catholics taking seriously the Beatitude: "Blessed are the poor in spirit, for theirs is the kingdom of heaven."

Our responsibility, then, ultimately resolves itself down to this: We are not sent into the world to preach social Revolution but *to be* the Revolution; we are not to envisage ourselves always as crucified but sometimes through our neglect as the Crucifiers. We must

realize that it is our duty to be supermen, that is, spiritual, and as apostles of God who is a consuming fire,
to enkindle fires in the souls of men and to give our
fellow men not only the *means* of existence but what
is vastly more important the *purpose* of existence. We
must realize furthermore that pacts and planning are
no substitute for moral force, and that we are not living only to preserve the *status quo* of a social order
which is already crumbling, but to supply the moral
convictions without which social order becomes disorder and chaos. In a word, the best way to reform the
world is to begin by reforming ourselves. The world
is in such a state of confusion and panic that it knows
not which road to take. It therefore will do no good
for us to shout: "Take the road that leads to religion.
Go to the Cross! Go to Christ!" The world is to be-
wildered that it will not go. But it will follow. That
means we must *go first*. An that is the way our Lord
led us. "Come — Follow Me!"

This implies our responsibility is of a redemptive
character. An analogy of our redemptive duty to the
world may be found in the triple vows of poverty,
chastity, and obedience. Why is there a vow of poverty
in the Church? Because wealth is bad? Wealth is not
necessarily an evil, for a rich man can exchange his
wealth for the kingdom of God. Why then the vow of
poverty? Because there are some souls in the world
who seek wealth as the be-all and the end-all here, and
there must needs be some who will "bend back" in the

other direction, and establish an equilibrium by aton-
ing for those who have wealth and know not how to
use it.

Why the vow of chastity? Because flesh is wrong?
No the flesh is not wrong; it may be elevated to the
dignity of the Sacrament. Why, then, the vow of
chastity? In order that through reparation and absti-
nence from even its legitimate pleasures of flesh atone-
ment might be made for those who indulge in its
excesses.

Why the vow of obedience? Because freedom is
wrong? There is nothing wrong about liberty. In fact
our will is the only thing that is really our own and
is, therefore, the most perfect gift that we can give to
God. Why then the vow of obedience? Because there
are men and women in the world who use their will
to sin, and they must be redeemed by those who are
willing to surrender it, to purchase for sinners the
glorious liberty of the children of God.

What these vows are to the Church in particular,
that we are to the world in general — its redeemers,
its leaven, and its salvation by and through the sacrifice of Christ on the Cross. We are our brother's
keeper; willing, therefore, we must be to suffer for
the sake of the community of souls of which we are
members, and to bear others' burdens as Christ has
borne ours. Naturally such a spirit of sacrifice and
responsibility toward the marginal Christians and the
masses which makes us willing to pray and sacrifice for

them requires the Spirit of Fortitude — a fortitude which transfigures us into redeemers with a small "r" as Christ was a Redeemer with a capital "R"; a fortitude which inspires us to bring our lives as wheat and grapes to be ground and crushed as bread and wine on the great altar of Calvary; a fortitude which recognizes that the triumph of evil cannot be complete, for the Captain of our salvation has already conquered the world.

Such a fortitude will not convert the world; it will not abolish all evil; it will not entirely deplete our bread lines; it will not do away with all wars and all injustices; it will not blot off the face of the earth the blood of the race of Cain; it will not stop every aching body and console every broken heart; it will not make everyone rich but it will do one thing — *it will save the world for this generation.*

The choice is clear: either the world will have a Revolution of Violence or a Revolution of Love. The Revolution of Love cannot just be preached, it must be lived by souls enkindled as the burning heart of Christ. Those of us who believe and live the Revolution of Love have only one objection against the Revolution of Violence, which means we have only one basic objection against Communism — it is not revolutionary enough. It leaves hate in the soul of man!